HUNTING
with
FERRETS

David Bezzant

THE CROWOOD PRESS

First published in 2008 by
The Crowood Press Ltd
Ramsbury, Marlborough
Wiltshire SN8 2HR

www.crowood.com

British Library Cataloguing-in-Publication Data
A catalogue record for this book is available from the British
Library.

ISBN 978 1 84797 005 3

Disclaimer
The author and the publisher do not accept any
responsibility in any manner whatsoever for any error or
omission, nor any loss, damage, injury or liability of any
kind incurred as a result of the use of any of the information
contained in this book, or reliance upon it.

Line artworks by Keith Field

Typeset in New Century Schoolbook by Bookcraft Ltd,
Stroud, Gloucestershire

Printed and bound in Malaysia by Times Offset (M) Sdn Bhd

CONTENTS

PREFACE

My brother and I were sitting at the kitchen table when our first ferrets arrived. Two mean-looking albinos, evidently past the first flush of youth, were delivered by a young gamekeeper who was immaculately dressed in matching tweed cap, jacket, waistcoat and plus twos. He charged the modest sum of one pound per ferret and wished us the best of luck. It was a good six weeks, including several bitten fingers, before the ferrets, a hob and a jill named Willie and Daisy respectively, agreed to an armistice and exchanged their hostile behaviour for more congenial conduct.

With their taming accomplished, we turned our attention to using the ferrets for the job that they have been associated with for several hundred years – hunting rabbits. Armed with snippets of information from several books, the counsel of an elderly neighbour, an assortment of cheap nets connected to oddly shaped homemade pegs, a carrying box crudely fashioned out of scrap wood and, of course, the two reformed ferrets, we set out enthusiastically in search of rabbits on the farmland near our home. Despite a couple of false starts, feelings of dejection, and weary aching limbs, we persevered and finally caught our first rabbit. I do not think that either of us will ever forget the feeling of excitement and sense of satisfaction that we experienced as the rabbit bolted into one of the purse nets that we had so carefully set. Even the ferret seemed pleased with his work. After several more successful outings we were well and truly hooked.

Soon we had found a variety of sites to hunt on, tracked down some top-quality handmade nets, smartened up our carrying boxes and taken on board the advice generously offered by elderly ferreters. We also added a new member to our ferreting team in the form of a roguish-looking terrier. He was full of instinct and ready for work.

More than twenty years have elapsed since then, during which time I have hunted in England, Wales and Scotland using a succession of working ferrets. Sometimes the work has been easy, with innumerable rabbits bolting into the nets as soon as the ferret goes to ground, while on other occasions the perseverance of the ferret, terrier and myself has been tested to the limit in order not to return home empty handed. I will never tire of watching a working ferret busying itself around a warren or of hearing that distinctive drumming of the rabbit's feet against the ground, which indicates that the rabbit is on the move and an impending bolt can be expected.

I have resisted the temptation to become involved with other field sports in order to concentrate on pursuing rabbits with ferrets and terriers. This book is based upon my experiences and describes the skills that I have developed and the methods that I employ to catch rabbits. I hope it does justice to this rural pastime by showing that hunting rabbits with ferrets is a sport that is cheap and simple to learn, exciting to practise and of sufficient interest to last a lifetime.

CHAPTER 1

WHY FERRETS ARE USED TO HUNT RABBITS

Since the rabbit settled in Britain during the 12th century it has been hunted in one way or another. Ferreting was amongst the earliest methods used to catch rabbits, and has been undertaken at various times and for different reasons by people of widely different social classes. Understanding the reasons why noblemen and noblewomen, tenant farmers and poachers used ferrets will give us a fairly accurate indication of why people choose to pursue this traditional pastime today. The primary reasons why ferreting has been practised continuously for many centuries can be divided into the following categories:

- to control the population of rabbits and thereby limit the damage that they cause
- to provide food
- to provide the rural dweller with a sporting interest that is enjoyable and humane
- to give ferrets the chance to employ their instinctive hunting abilities.

Today's ferreter may identify with one of the above reasons as the incentive for his regular hunting excursions, or he may be influenced in part by all of them. Whichever is the case, all these reasons warrant more careful examination.

Controlling the Rabbit Population

Farmers and rabbits have been antagonists for hundreds of years. The first person to give me permission to hunt on his land was a Cambridgeshire arable farmer. He was a tiny man who hid his thinning hair under a trilby hat, which he wore constantly. He was a straightforward character, not noted for spontaneous outbursts of enthusiasm. We were, therefore, totally astounded by the keenness with which our enquiry concerning ferreting was met and the speed with which he welcomed us as newfound allies in his struggle to avoid half-nibbled crops.

British farmers probably thought that they had seen the last of the rabbit following the introduction of myxomatosis to England in 1953. Although the disease quickly spread to all parts of the UK, resulting in horrendous suffering and a dramatic depletion in numbers, the rabbit managed to survive. Today, the rabbit remains as inextricably linked with the farming community as it did hundreds of years ago.

The rabbit had been in the UK for 600 years before it was recognized as not only a nuisance, but a real threat to the farmers' livelihood. On a 1300-acre estate in Kirkcaldy, the annual damage attributed to rabbits was recorded over a 5-year period and ranged from £428 in 1839 to £655 in 1841, reaching its height in 1844 at £1000.

A ferreter from the 1940s. Large numbers of rabbits could be caught regularly and sold for a reasonable price.

No tenant farmer at that time could view, without misgiving, rabbits destroying his crops, which could result in a financial loss of 50–80 pence per acre. The widespread distribution and massive proliferation of rabbits that took place during the 19th century is ironically attributed to advances in farming practice and the associated improvement of land. Prior to this there were many counties, most notably in Scotland, where rabbits were not commonly seen, even as late as 1810.

During the 19th century the majority of farms were in the ownership of aristocratic families. As a consequence of the Game Laws, the tenant farmers who rented the land and properties had no legal right to catch rabbits, irrespective of the damage they caused, unless they could first secure the permission of their landlords. The Act of 1621 decreed that only owners of ploughgates of land, reckoned to be about 130 acres, could kill game of any kind and Parliament, in which the landed interests were firmly entrenched, passed even stricter laws, such as the Night Poaching Act of 1829 and the Game Act of 1832. Most landlords chose to ignore the pleas of the hardworking tenants for some measure of rabbit control. This was so that they could establish enormous sporting estates overflowing with game, which they and their guests could hunt for entertainment. Inevitably, the dispute became quite bitter on both sides and effigies of prominent figures, with rabbits hanging from their coat tails, were burnt when feelings were running high. A number of trenchant articles were published, urging for a reform of the Game Laws. Finally, the Commons voted in favour of the Ground Game Act of 1881.

The Ground Game Act gave tenant farmers the legal right to control rabbits living on the land they rented. In so doing, Parliament resisted the pressure of many influential families by identifying the farmers' right to safeguard their livelihood as more important than the Squire's desire for sport. The statute also clearly showed that a population of rabbits, when left unchecked, was capable of reducing the growth of a crop to such a level that the living of the farmer was threatened. From that point on, people of more humble origins were able to hunt rabbits, and they made use of a variety of methods including traps, snares, dogs and ferrets. Subsequent Acts, such as the Prevention of Damage by Rabbits Act passed in 1939, went a step further and empowered local authorities so that they could compel both landowners and occupiers to kill rabbits in order to prevent the destruction of land and crops.

Farming has undergone great change since the 19th century, but the rabbit, with its desire to eat farmed crops and graze upon prized pastureland, remains an annoying 'thorn in the flesh' to farmers and those whose livelihood relies on the growth of vegetation, flowers, grassland and, in some cases, forestry. Today, it is unlikely that a burgeoning rabbit population could literally eat a farmer out of

business, but many would agree that farmers have a legal and moral right to try to minimize the damage that rabbits undoubtedly do.

Experienced gamekeepers and traditional pest controllers consider ferreting to be the best natural method of reducing rabbit numbers, and the ferreter is a welcome visitor on most farms. The ferreter will obviously want to hunt in successive years on the land he has access to, and will therefore aim to reduce stock levels only as far as is necessary to mitigate crop damage. In my experience, farmers have found no notable loss of crops or grass after I have used my ferrets to reduce rabbit numbers by between 70 and 90 per cent. In fact, they are often surprised when I tell them how many rabbits they still have left on their land. Ferreting does not advocate killing every rabbit in sight. Instead, it offers a long-term systematic programme of controlling rabbit numbers, which keeps landowners happy and ferreters occupied, and also acknowledges the rabbit's right to exist as a species and the valuable position it holds in the countryside.

Provision of Food

The American hunter Sam Fadala, in his book entitled *A Complete Guide to Game Care and Cookery*, alludes to the fact that, for a lot of people, the greatest thrill in hunting is the taking home of fresh meat that is caught and not bought and is from a wild as opposed to a farmed source. He suggests that this is self-sufficiency in its truest sense.

I believe that a lot of ferreters in this country identify with such sentiments and, like me, will admit to taking a certain amount of pride in being able to catch their

own food. During my early days of ferreting, it was a family custom to have rabbit
that had been caught on Saturday for
Sunday dinner. My mother would blow the
dust off her collection of antiquated cookbooks so that she could experiment with
weird and wonderful recipes. The caught
rabbits cost nothing but hard work and are
killed quickly and humanely. Add this to
the ferreter's knowledge of where his catch
comes from and what it feeds upon, and
his control of the butchering and prepara-
tion of the meat, and wild rabbit becomes
a hard deal to ignore or better.

However, the majority of the population
in the UK today does not agree with this
view, and wild rabbit is not a significant
part of the national diet. Furthermore,
most people have never tasted wild rabbit,
and there is a definite lack of desire to
eat it. I find it surprising and a little dis-
appointing when farmers and their wives
turn down the offer of a free rabbit that
has been caught on their land, often with
the explanation that they would not know
what to do with it in terms of either its
skinning and jointing or cooking. Sometimes this may be an excuse, so that they
can refuse without causing offence, but on
one occasion I could not persuade a landowner to take a couple of rabbits even for
dog food.

Wild rabbit meat was not always held in
such low regard and was eaten regularly by
a wide variety of people up until the 1950s.
So what has changed? It could be argued
that myxomatosis led to the disappearance
of rabbit on the menu. Not only did it wipe
out nearly all the rabbits, it also presented
a completely new image of the rabbit, which
was as a sick and diseased animal. As a
result, the meat was considered contami-
nated and inedible. This image remained
uppermost in people's minds even when

the rabbit showed a marked recovery from
the disease. In addition, changes in lifestyle
and shopping behaviour, combined with the
widespread availability of cheap farmed
meat, meant that wild rabbit was destined
to never again regain its popularity.

However, are we really missing out, or
was rabbit meat only ever peasants' food
eaten as a matter of necessity rather than
choice? It is recorded that the occurrence
of butchered meat on the menu was a sign
of social status enjoyed by the wealthier
tradesmen and their supposed betters
during the 19th century. The poor had a
rather grim diet, consisting of potatoes,
oatmeal and milk dishes, and it is not difficult to imagine that rabbit meat would
have been a welcome relief. Old cookbooks
are amongst the most reliable commentar-
ies on eating behaviour at the time of their
publication. They present us with a good
idea of the value that was placed upon
rabbit meat as an ingredient and even who
the meal would have been intended for. A
cookbook published in 1905 records that
the plain English way of cooking rabbit,
such as in a pie, was reserved for those
below stairs, while estate owners and their
shooting guests would have been served
a dish that was influenced by French
cuisine.

Most cookbooks written during the 19th
and 20th centuries feature between three
and five recipes that use rabbit as the principal ingredient. This highlights the fact
that wild rabbit was eaten regularly and,
when cooked with care and imagination,
was considered to be both appetizing and
tasty. For example, the real Mrs Bridges,
who was later to be immortalized in the
drama *Upstairs, Downstairs*, made what
she called 'Southwold Rabbit Pie' with
rabbits caught by Pegler the warrener and
his ferrets. In a cookbook that she wrote in

a similar style to the better-known *Mrs Beeton's Cookbook*, she states that her rabbit pie was always a favourite of the staff and was even appreciated by the tastebuds of her upper-crust employers.

Going back further in time, to the 13th century, we find that rabbit held a prominent place on the tables of monarch and nobleman alike, with the most notable case being King Henry III who, during a Christmas feast, had no fewer than 500 hares and 200 rabbits on the menu. Two hundred years later, at the installation of George Neville as Chancellor of England, the menu included 4000 rabbits. Consequently, throughout the years, rabbit has been a meat for all strata of society, and there remain to this day recipes that are capable of impressing the most discerning eater.

Having established the fact that rabbit can taste good, it is worth pointing out that it is also good for you. As long ago as 1972, research conducted at the University of Alaska proved that game meat is better for a person's health than farmed meat. This is mainly because it contains much less fat, and it is the consumption of fatty food that has been linked with high cholesterol and plaque formations in arteries, leading to strokes and heart attacks. Sam Fadala, in his *Complete Guide to Game Care and Cookery*, relates a story about a friend who was told to reduce his intake of foodstuffs high in cholesterol. Thinking that this meant all meat, he was disgruntled because, as he admitted to the doctor, he had a freezer full of game meat. 'Oh, that's different,' the doctor exclaimed. He went on to inform him that it is possible to eat more wild meat than domestic meat and still maintain a healthy cholesterol level.

Not only is rabbit far lower in fat, it also contains at least one-third more protein and more vitamin A, thiamine, riboflavin and niacin than farmed alternatives. As small game, rabbit is given organic status and there is no risk of chemical interference such as antibiotic treatment or growth promoters. There is a growing concern about meat production and welfare standards, and traceability is a key word coined by the top chefs of today. None of this will trouble the ferreter because he knows precisely where his rabbit comes from, what it fed upon and how and when it was killed.

The value of small game is often overlooked today. I believe that the rabbit, which is still quite plentiful in the British countryside, deserves a place on our plates for the reasons already stated, and there is no more enjoyable way to get some fresh rabbits for the pot than to spend a couple of hours ferreting.

An Enjoyable and Humane Sporting Interest

In years gone by, if you were brought up in the countryside, you would probably have had a go at ferreting during your childhood or have known somebody in the village who used ferrets. During my grandfather's generation, ferreting was second only to fishing as the rural lad's favourite outdoor hobby. Even the elite pupils of Eton, Harrow and Rugby were encouraged to learn about hunting with ferrets, as evidenced by the book entitled *Studies in the Art of Rat Catching – With Additional Notes on Ferrets and Ferreting, Rabbiting and Long Netting*, which was written by H.C. Barkley in 1911 specifically for public-school boys.

A contemporary ferreter employs essentially the same technique as those people who first practised the sport in Britain nearly 800 years ago.

If we go back further, to the very earliest days of ferreting, we discover that the nobility were the leading exponents of the sport and, in all likelihood, the majority of early ferreters would have been wealthy women who viewed the hunting of rabbits solely as a source of entertainment.

Clearly, throughout the span of eight centuries, people of different ages and backgrounds have enjoyed the use of ferrets to catch rabbits. I do not think that ferreting would be as popular today if it were considered to be an excessively cruel form of rabbit control. It is a reality of modern life that most field sports are subject to a certain amount of public scrutiny, and for this reason I wish to point out why ferreting can claim to be one of the most humane ways of controlling rabbits.

Traditional ferreting is seasonal and not practised during the warmer months of the year. This is primarily to allow the rabbit to breed undisturbed when conditions for its survival are at their best. It also prevents the capture of immature rabbits, which lack sufficient bodyweight for the purpose of eating. Furthermore, research has shown that ferreting and rabbit shooting in winter has a greater effect on reducing the population than at any other time of the year.

Caught rabbits are killed instantly. The ferreter ensures that there is no delay and, apart from one deliberate blow to break the neck, the handling of the rabbit when it is in the net does not inflict pain. The experienced hunter is so quick and decisive in his actions that there is literally no time for the rabbit to panic.

Ferreted rabbit is killed for a purpose, which is to provide food for humans, dogs and ferrets. Some enthusiasts even treat the skins, so that no part of the animal is wasted. The Americans aptly refer to people who hunt with this intention as game meat harvesters.

As well as being humane, ferreting may be regarded as a sport in the truest sense of the word for the following reasons. Firstly, rabbits remain genuinely wild animals and are wary of human beings. As such, their survival instincts are not relaxed for a moment, which means that they will use all their considerable energies to evade capture. Secondly, although ferreters learn to be thorough, there is always an element of chance that can favour the rabbit. For instance, bolt holes may be overlooked and nets can malfunction. When working some warrens that terminate under rock mounds or corrugated tin, it is sometimes only possible to cover half the number of bolt holes satisfactorily with nets. In such cases, the likelihood of the rabbit finding an escape is much higher. Thirdly, the ferreter has an affinity for the rabbit owing to the fact that he gets to know its habits and ways better than any other hunter. It is hoped that this traditional method of rabbit control will prevent numbers getting too high and so avoid resorting to strict forms of pest control that have no regard for the continuance of the rabbit. In conclusion, the ferreter enjoys his sport, possesses genuine respect for the rabbit and offers a long-term, humane and viable way to manage the growth of the rabbit population.

Providing the Ferret with the Opportunity to Hunt

Anyone who has worked ferrets will know that they are ideally suited to hunting rabbits and evidently enjoy doing so. It is a job that they have been bred and trained for.

The typical characteristics of predatory animals, such as lively senses, patience, determination, stamina, agility and courage, are all possessed by the ferret and, when combined with its instinctive drive at the warren, result in a formidable and very efficient hunter. Ferrets, like working terriers, have an ingrained knowledge of how to handle themselves in the subterranean environment and are probably at their happiest when underground and on the scent of a rabbit. Time

Hunting rabbits in a warren can be hard work, but ferrets thrive on it.

and again I have seen one of my ferrets appear at the opening of a bolt hole and turn around swiftly as it pursues a rabbit that is doing its best to evade it. The look of determination on its face and dedication to its task are plain to see; every expression and movement shows that it is intent on its work.

My ferrets do not resist any aspect of rabbiting and, thankfully, do not resent me for sticking them down narrow dark tunnels. This activity satisfies the ferret's instinctive desire to hunt and, in addition, stimulates its senses, makes it think and exercises its body in a manner that no other activity can compare with. The result is an alert, content, fit and extremely healthy ferret. I also like to think that the ferret

Ferrets are ideally built for rapid movement through warrens and are quick to develop an awareness of nets.

A ferreter kitted out for a day's hunting.

derives some pleasure from being in the company of its owner.

Regular hunting is good for the ferret, and the genuine ferreter places such a high value upon his working ferrets that he would shudder at the thought of doing anything that harmed them. Without doubt, ferrets are of inestimable use to the ardent rabbit hunter, and these fearless little animals relish every opportunity that they are given to put their instinctive talents to the test.

Reasons for Ferreting

- To prevent damage to valuable crops and pasture
- To keep rabbit numbers at an acceptable level
- To harvest healthy meat free of charge
- To continue a traditional country pursuit that is enjoyable, inexpensive, non-exclusive and easy to practise irrespective of age or gender
- Traditional ferreting is seasonal and, as a result, balances control with conservation

---

CHAPTER 2

WHAT EVERY FERRETER SHOULD KNOW ABOUT RABBITS

Native peoples throughout the world, who have relied on successful hunting expeditions for their survival, collectively abide by the principle that if you choose to hunt an animal you should first get to know its ways so that you can understand its behaviour and correctly interpret the signs and tracks that it leaves. It is a principle that is relevant to all forms of present-day hunting, especially ferreting. The ferreter needs to know some very specific details about the rabbit, which fall into the following categories:

• the rabbit's abode – the warren
• the rabbit's habits
• tell-tale signs left by rabbits
• the physical handling of wild rabbits.

Before we look at these in more detail, it would be interesting to ascertain how the rabbit first came to Britain.

It was thought that the Normans introduced the rabbit into England initially. However, there are no written records of the rabbit until 1176, which has resulted in the belief that the Crusaders brought the rabbit to these shores in the late 12th century. Details remain scarce and there is some uncertainty about whether this rabbit was one that had been domesticated by the monks on the continent or whether it was from captive wild stock.

The rabbits were kept by the wealthy in enormous enclosures called warrens, which extended to thousands of acres. Employed professionals, aptly known as warreners, who literally lived among the rabbits and managed the land so that it was rabbit-friendly, maintained these warrens. Given time and taking into account the rabbit's determination, it was inevitable that there would be escapees. These free rabbits quickly made themselves at home in the countryside and, as each century passed, they moved further northwards and westwards until they occupied Wales and Scotland as well. They have had much to contend with, but they have, to a large extent, triumphed over their adversaries and remain very much a part of the countryside. When hunting, the ferreter spends most of his time at the warren, and it is to this that we now turn our attention.

THE WARREN

The ferreter catches rabbits at the warren. Consequently, he needs to know these structures inside out. Rabbit warrens are not subject to planning permission or building inspection and therefore there is no such thing as a standard warren. These homes are literally scraped out of the earth at the rabbit's inclination; its instincts prompt this behaviour. Just like our homes, rabbit warrens can be large or small, set in wonderfully picturesque surrounds or overlooking a rubbish dump. They may date back hundreds of years or be freshly dug.

Warrens are essentially a network of underground tunnels, most commonly approximating 10in (25cm) in diameter throughout their length with the entrances being generally larger. The rabbit is a skilful miner and can hollow out tunnels in the hardest of grounds and direct them through obstacles, such as under trees and along hedge bottoms, in a way that a structural engineer would have difficulty matching. Whether the land is as flat as a pancake or as steep as Everest, this versatile animal can shovel the soil aside to make a comfortable home.

The intention of all this digging is to provide the rabbit with shelter from the weather and a place to rest and breed that is safe from predators. Because the warren is recessed into the earth, it provides a warm environment for the rabbit even during the worst spells of weather. It is also very effective at protecting the rabbit from a number of its enemies that are unable to pursue the rabbit underground. Admittedly, the stoat, polecat and ferret can make their way easily through a warren but, seeming to foresee this danger, the

Uncultivated ground that borders agricultural land is an ideal place for rabbits to reside.

Rabbits often dig their warrens at the base of hedges. Here nets are set along the bottom of a gorse hedge.

circumspect rabbit has tipped the scales positively in its favour by ensuring that there are a number of holes that it can choose to bolt from. In the best warrens the rabbit builders have been particularly clever and provided themselves with a hidden bolt hole some distance away from the main warren, and these have been known to catch out the careful net setter. They are dug in a similar way to the tunnels in *The Great Escape*, from underground to the surface, so as not to give themselves away with the tell-tale little mounds of earth that are so apparent when the chamber is dug from the outside in.

At most of the locations that I have hunted, the rabbits rarely limit themselves to just one warren or a warren that is only just big enough for them. They prefer to

keep their options open and usually have a choice of warrens to bolt to when they feel threatened. It is not unusual for warrens that are spaced apart and seemingly unrelated to be used by the same rabbits depending upon which they are closest to when they are alarmed.

Rabbits are sociable animals and a large colony will inhabit an equally large warren, which they have jointly excavated and which requires a bag full of purse nets to cover. Alternatively, a number of smaller warrens lying side by side along a hedgerow may be used. In some situations it can be difficult to determine where one warren ends and another starts or even if they are indeed separate warrens. When working warrens that you do not know the extent of, the most logical course of action is to net all the holes at the outset. Even if all the holes do not combine to form one large warren, you will not have wasted your time. It will enable you to progress from one warren to another in quick succession. Another benefit with this approach becomes apparent if a rabbit bolts from the warren you are working and slips a net. Invariably the rabbit will make for the nearest safe haven, which has already been netted, and so the rabbit is caught as it flees into the warren.

For the purpose of the ferreter, a warren may be described in practical terms as any location that a rabbit uses as a temporary or permanent residence, which can be covered with purse nets and to which the ferret can be entered. Some such locations,

for example a mound of dumped concrete blocks or the abandoned roof of a chicken shed, clearly do not resemble the typical warren, but I have chosen to classify them under the same heading because the same process is used to work them. The rabbits often opt for these makeshift shelters during the time of day when the ferreter is most likely to be hunting and, as I have learnt, this is quite a prudent move because they have a much greater chance of escape owing to the precarious way some of the nets have to be positioned.

Rabbits make use of the strangest materials to provide themselves with a safe shelter. I have noticed on several occasions when working farm sites that rabbits think nothing of squeezing through coils of

Rabbits need shelter and they will make use of features such as this stone wall to protect their warren from the weather.

wire or crawling on their stomachs under corrugated tin in order to place themselves in a safe position. They are capable of incorporating these abandoned materials into a network of tunnels that are barely discernible to the human eye and can be easily overlooked. The rabbit is a creative creature; a mound of rocks can become a system of tunnels with only a small amount of industry on its behalf. The warren is clearly the rabbit's fortress and it should be approached with the respect that a stronghold deserves.

The ferreter must become an expert at recognizing rabbit warrens, since this is where all his hunting efforts are concentrated. Familiarity with these structures also enables him to avoid confusing them with the home of that other renowned occupant of the underground world – the badger. At first sight, it may appear that the rabbit warren and badger sett share some fundamental similarities. However, as a general rule, the chambers of a sett are considerably larger than the tunnels of a warren. I have encountered some warrens where the bolt holes are large enough for my terrier to enter easily, and it is these that can cause some confusion. In such cases the ferreter should rely on the signs that a badger leaves in the vicinity of the sett for correct identification. The Fell and Moorland Working Terrier Club take this identification very seriously owing to both the legal and working repercussions of making a mistake. They list six signs to look out for:

1. Badger tracks, i.e. pad marks.
2. Signs of bedding near the sett entrances.
3. Regular paths to dung pits.
4. Scratches and claw marks at the base of nearby trees.
5. Coarse grey hairs with black near tip, often caught in barbed wire, briars or low trees near the sett.
6. Signs of excavation linked by well-defined paths.

If any of these signs are present, the ferreter should stay away because it is an offence under the Consolidated Badgers Act of 1993 to interfere with a sett in any way. The identification of a warren or sett becomes like a sixth sense to the experienced ferreter.

THE RABBIT'S HABITS

Knowing how rabbits spend their day and where they are likely to be at different times is of enormous benefit to the hunter. Contemporary ferreters probably need to understand rabbit behaviour better than those who hunted in the pre-myxomatosis era, because the rabbits are not as widely spread as they once were and therefore not as easy to catch.

Essentially, life for the mature rabbit when it is not in a warren is like being on permanent sentry duty. It is an innately cautious creature and its nose, ears and eyes are on constant alert to the threat of danger. When it does detect an imminent threat, it will either sprint to the nearest warren at breakneck speed using paths that it travels every day or, alternatively, if the rabbit feels that it has not been spotted, it may remain where it is and hide by crouching low to the ground.

Although all rabbits behave in a common way, external pressures such as geographical location, the availability of food, geological make-up of the land and the weather will prompt the rabbits to conduct themselves in a fashion that best suits their

(a)

(b)

(c)

Field sketches of rabbits showing: (a) a rabbit feeding; (b) a rabbit on the alert; (c) a rabbit crouching in long grass in an effort to avoid being noticed.

is hunting in and think about the ways in which it may influence the rabbits' behaviour:

- What kind of cover is available for the rabbit and will it encourage or discourage them from staying on the surface during the day?
- Where can the rabbits make their home – are there hedges, woodlands, ditches or scrubland?
- Where and what is the most likely source of food for the rabbit?
- What is the land used for – is there a lot of human activity that will scare the rabbits?

Rabbits are generally thought to be most active during the hours of darkness, which is welcomed as a form of protection, and it is during winter evenings, when shining a powerful torch across the fields, that I get my most regular sightings of rabbits. Done in a gradual arc, this does not startle them and I am able to observe them for a reasonable amount of time. They may sense its beam as the light illuminates their position and, initially, they may crouch low and hug the earth or stay absolutely still, but they soon relax if the light is kept in the same position. After a moment or two, they will happily return to feeding. Every so often a rabbit may kick out its hind legs and make a short dash in a zigzag formation, which is, I presume, its way of letting off steam or pent-up energy as well as stretching muscles that have been restrained within the confines of a warren. Watching the rabbits like this indicates how healthy and vigorous they are.

Rabbits that are seen in the open during daylight hours are usually either very young, sick, stupid or so confident in their surroundings that they do not feel threatened

surroundings. Therefore, rabbits at different locations may show variations in what they eat, where they spend their daylight hours and where they live.

Ancient sportsmen understood this and nicknamed the rabbits accordingly: 'warreners' obviously lived in warrens, 'parkers' preferred open ground and 'hedgehogs' dwelt in woodlands. The ferreter should observe the environment he or vulnerable. I watched a group of rabbits grow up in the field next to mine and, when they were very young, I often got sight of at least four of them munching nonchalantly on the grass. At first they did not seem to notice me standing watching them, but the older they got the more alert and cautious they became. I believe that rabbits spend a lot more time out of the warren than we think. Our assumption is that if the rabbit cannot be seen, it must be underground, but this overlooks the rabbit's mastery of disguise. Give the rabbit some long grass, the base of an overgrown hedge or even a mound of rocks and it can merge with its surroundings like a chameleon so that it is barely visible. I am sure that rabbits enjoy being in the fresh air and feeling the sun's rays, but they will remain within a fixed territory and always have a safe retreat.

The primary incentive for the rabbit being above ground is to feed. The menu is strictly vegetarian, with grass being the main meal. It is supplemented by most types of vegetable and herb, some weeds and, in cases of extreme weather, the bark of young trees. Unlike humans, once the rabbit's stomach is full it can stay that way for a number of days owing to the fact that the food passes through the digestive system twice. This process is known as refection and is both a survival aid and a defence mechanism since it limits the amount of time that the rabbit has to spend outside the warren, which is when it is most vulnerable.

The rabbit world, like the human one, is an organized social structure in which shared company is commonplace. Certain characters occupy positions of dominance within the community and, without exception, the leader will be a large mature buck. However, he does not rule his empire with a rod of iron and only becomes a bit fractious during the breeding season. His prominent position gives him the choice of the best rooms within the warren, the best feeding ground and the pick of the ladies. He also has his responsibilities, the most important being to protect his community. He does this primarily by patrolling his territory, which can range from just over half an acre up to fifteen acres, leaving little smelly messages to ward off strangers. This is done by depositing secretions on the ground by rubbing his chin backwards and forwards upon it.

It would appear that the does are the brains behind the community, because the design and construction of the warrens is almost all their handiwork. The language of the rabbit is contained within aromatic scents released by secreting glands and in urine. It is this strong sense of smell that enables the rabbits to identify the individual members of their community as well as the presence of any strangers.

One of the reasons for its persecution and also survival is the breeding potential of the rabbit. In a single year one may become thirty, although it is unlikely that all the offspring will survive. The defined breeding season is from February to late July, but the breeding is more intense and the survival rate of kits much greater during the warmer weather. Given a gestation period of 30 days followed by approximately 25 days in the nest, infant rabbits first appear towards the end of March.

The pregnant doe creates a special breeding chamber, which is typically a short tunnel with only one exit point. This is known as a 'stop', and the doe will line the furthest recess with grass, dead plants and tufts of fur, which she moulds into a nest. On rare occasions a doe may use the offshoot of a warren instead of digging a

A baby rabbit with typically rounded features.

'stop'. Although the newborns rely totally on the mother for their survival, she does not remain with them constantly and only returns to the nest once every 24h for a short period of suckling. She does this for the first 3–4 weeks of the kits' lives, after which they are left to fend for themselves. Invariably the baby rabbits find their way to the main warren and join the large established family of older rabbits.

It is estimated that during their upbringing the mother spends as little as 2–3min each day with her kits, and this behaviour, known aptly as 'absentee care', is thought to be a way of protecting the young by not drawing attention to them. If the ferreter discovers a 'stop', he should not enter his ferret to it.

TELL-TALE SIGNS LEFT BY RABBITS

The rabbit leaves some very clear indicators of its presence in the countryside, and experienced countrymen are able to read these signs as clearly as signposts. They indicate where rabbits live, how far their territory extends, where they feed and the paths they travel from the warren to the feeding ground. Some signs are more obvious than others but, with practice, the eye of a person can become nearly as informative as the nose of a bloodhound.

It is very rare for a person to be able to see the imprint of the individual paws of the rabbit on the ground. This is because they are small and the rabbit is very light on its feet. Rabbits also do not favour walking over ground upon which a footprint would be easily seen, such as mud. Therefore, do not rely on paw prints to lead you to inhabited rabbit warrens. You may be lucky and see the odd one here and there, which will prove that you are on the right track. The exception to this is during snow, when continuous uniform depressions are the tell-tale sign of the rabbits' hind feet. As a resident of Scotland, I probably get more opportunity than most to observe such

An unmistakable sign of rabbits is a narrow, well-worn path in long grass.

tracks in the snow. They are easy to follow, although they can become so numerous and criss-cross over one another so often near the warren that they are impossible to tell apart.

Rabbits tend to use the same paths over and over again, which results in a trail that is distinguishable either by the thinning or balding of the grass or, when the grass is longer, by a hollow run. These pathways tend to be about 3in (8cm) wide and can be seen from a distance, allowing the hunter to take an overview of the field and pinpoint clearly the rabbit's route as it moves from one location to another, usually terminating in the vicinity of the warren. Even when a rabbit is startled and flees at speed it will, if it can, follow one of these established paths. Typically, they lead to areas that afford the rabbit some cover or where it can disappear underground. Identifying these paths enables the ferreter to literally walk in the rabbit's footsteps and, by doing so, get a feel for its domain. This, as we shall see later, is of enormous benefit when hunting the rabbit in certain circumstances.

Equally familiar sights left by the rabbit are pellets or droppings. These are round, sultana-sized and usually left in clusters in very shallow depressions in the earth. However, I have noticed such clusters on the tops of old bales and even on large rocks.

It might look like the product of loutish behaviour, but the depositing of droppings in a seemingly random fashion is akin to a human putting up a fence – they mark the boundary of the rabbits' territory. This communicates the message to strange rabbits from outside the colony that they had either best stay away or be on their best behaviour, which means showing subservience to the resident dominant buck.

Within the territory where rabbits are active you will notice indiscriminate diggings or shallow scrapings in the ground. No one knows why rabbits scrape away at the earth like this, but the most popular suggestion is that they are seeking to supplement their diet with some essential ingredients from the grass or plants that they uproot. I favour this option for two reasons. Firstly, the rabbit is guided by its instincts and there are far too many scrapings for them to be an accident or serve no purpose. Secondly, I have noticed our ponies eating grass roots, which they harvest by pawing a front hoof at the ground repeatedly. The resulting indentation is very similar to the scraping left by a rabbit.

The most obvious sign of the presence of rabbits is a warren. The ferreter now has to figure out if the warren is in use or not. As my brother and I have found out, a large and impressive-looking warren is not necessarily in use. If the ferreter has not seen rabbits bolting into a warren he must look for the above-mentioned signs in order to confirm that the warren is active.

A worthwhile companion to the ferreter is a suitable dog which, when properly trained, is capable of pinpointing exactly where rabbits are to be found by utilizing its amazing scenting powers. On the day of the hunt, the working dog will be able to indicate with remarkable accuracy those warrens that have rabbits in, and those that do not. This is of great benefit to the ferreter. The correct employment of my terrier brings a whole new dimension to my search for rabbits.

Signs of Rabbits

- Distinctive footprints and tracks in soft ground
- Narrow rabbit runs in grass
- Shallow random diggings
- Rabbit droppings
- Small amounts of fur caught on fences and hedges
- Communal latrine
- System of interconnected tunnels terminating in a series of holes on the surface, otherwise known as a warren
- Actual sightings of rabbits – when they are young or feel very confident in their environment, it is possible to watch them

HANDLING WILD RABBITS

One of the important skills that a ferreter should possess is the ability to handle a wild rabbit confidently, including how to kill it quickly without hesitation. This is to prevent any unnecessary distress being caused to the rabbit, and to ensure that the caught rabbit does not escape.

I have watched some of the old ferreters at work, men who grew up before the Second World War when it was possible to catch a huge number of rabbits in a single day. Even though they are advanced in years, these sportsmen are able to pick up, kill and place a rabbit out of the way with an effortless speed. There is no fuss, no prevarication, no uncertainty and this is, without doubt, a result of familiarity with the animal and continual practice of the task. The best way to learn how to physically deal with wild rabbits is to watch somebody who is proficient at the task. You will learn how to kill a rabbit much more quickly by watching an expert for a short time and having a go under his supervision than by reading detailed descriptions in books. However, the ideal is not always possible and, in this case, there are now some good photographic depictions of this task being performed; they should be studied diligently in the absence of an instructor.

I believe that any hunter should possess a certain measure of respect for his quarry, irrespective of what it is. This manifests itself in all his dealings with the animal and most notably when he is physically handling it. I have spent enough time around a variety of animals to know that there is a right and a wrong way to approach and hold them. One sends them into a blind panic while the other keeps them relatively calm. Thoughtful handling should always be a top priority for the ferreter, not only for the sake of the animal itself, but also to avoid any risk of injury to himself arising from the rabbit kicking out its hind legs or, worse still, losing hold of the rabbit and allowing it to escape.

The most frequent occasion on which the ferreter is required to handle the rabbit is when it has bolted into a net at speed as it is driven from the warren by the ferret. As a result of shock, surprise or even surrender, the rabbit will lie still for a short time. This is when the ferreter should get hold of the rabbit, including the net. I always hold the rabbit with one hand around the loins; there are two reasons for this. Firstly, it appears to immobilize the rabbit and thereby prevents it struggling. Secondly, it stops the rabbit from using its primary defensive weapons – the hind feet.

Once the rabbit is caught it should be killed quickly without delay. There are three recognized methods of doing this – the chop, chin-up and stretch methods respectively – and their names accurately imply what they involve.

The chop method is easy to master. It uses the edge of the hand to deliver a blow to the posterior part of the rabbit's skull. In so doing the neck is cleanly broken and the animal dies instantly. People who think that this method requires a lot of force are misled; it is a matter of hitting the rabbit in the right position at the correct angle with a smooth downward stroke. The main advantage of this method is its versatility. Once it is mastered, the rabbit can be killed quickly while it is still in the net, and it can be employed with equal effect even when the ferreter is standing in some awkward positions. To summarize, the chop method involves the following steps:

1. Secure hold of the rabbit around the loins while it is still in the net.

2. Transfer the rabbit from the ground so that the paws of its front legs can be rested over your thigh. The rabbit is less inclined to panic when its paws are in contact with something rather than suspended in mid-air and the chop can be delivered with more precision.
3. Deliver a downward chop inclined sideward at forty-five degrees to the back of the skull.

From start to finish, this process is completed in a matter of seconds.

The chin-up method works in exactly the same way – by breaking the rabbit's neck – but employs a different technique. Once again, the method is easy to learn and can be used when the rabbit is still in the net. It involves the following steps:

1. Secure hold of the rabbit and the net.
2. Hold it against the ground, with one hand covering the front shoulder blades and lower neck.
3. With the other hand, grasp hold of the rabbit underneath the chin and pull this sharply upwards and backwards in a continuous movement.

The stretch method is slightly more complicated and there is a knack to it that some find difficult to master. The process is as follows:

1. Secure hold of the rabbit by the loins and remove it from the net that has pursed around it.
2. Hold the hind legs extended in one hand.
3. Place the second hand over the head of the rabbit by sliding it down the body.

4. The hands are now pulled in opposing directions and at the same time the hand over the head moves it sharply upwards in a similar fashion to the chin-up method.

I have used all of these methods and personally favour the straightforward chop. However, if you exert too much force or hit the wrong point when delivering the blow, you are likely to hurt your hand. For this reason I do not recommend it to younger ferreters. It is also the reason why I suggest you get somebody to show you how to do it. The chin-up method has much to recommend it and is the best option if you have to teach yourself from a book. It is reliable and there is no risk of injury to the hand. I have never liked the stretch method, essentially because the rabbit cannot be killed unless it is first removed from the net, which makes it slightly slower than the other methods.

The most important consideration is that you select the method that you are most comfortable with, and have confidence in, so that the rabbit is always killed at the first attempt. Whether you use the chop, chin-up or stretch technique to kill the rabbit, expect the body to twitch or convulse for a short time following dispatch. This is quite natural and does not mean that the rabbit is still alive. If you have any doubts, check the neck, which should feel flaccid or wobbly, and look at the ears, which should be at right angles to the body. As William Thomas points out in his book *Rabbit Shooting to Ferrets*, a live rabbit, when held in human hands, uses muscular control to lay its ears flat along its back, but when it is killed the ears immediately start to stand up due to the cessation of muscular control.

CHAPTER 3

HOW TO GET STARTED

Many people express an interest in a sport or pursuit, but do not follow it up owing to such obstacles as the cost of equipment and lessons. However, those who genuinely wish to take up ferreting need not be concerned by either the cost or the need for a lengthy course of lessons. It is an easy sport to take up and requires a minuscule budget. To hunt rabbits you need a ferret, some basic equipment and access to land where rabbits can be found. We now discuss each of these in more detail before illustrating how they combine when planning a day's rabbiting.

BUYING A FERRET

The ferret is the most important purchase that you will make. Without a fit and capable ferret, regardless of how expensive your equipment is or how much rabbit-inhabited land you have to hunt on, you will not catch anything. Every effort should be made to get the best ferret that you can.

Where to Look for a Ferret

Wherever you live, it should not be too difficult to find a ferret using one or more of the following sources:

- Local newspapers often advertise ferrets from working stock for sale.
- Local gamekeepers, even if they do not keep ferrets themselves, usually know somebody who does.
- Specialized publications dealing with field sports are available at newsagents, but the most useful for the ferreter is *The Countryman's Weekly*, which incorporates a weekly supplement devoted to terriers and working ferrets.
- Ferret organizations will help those with an interest in ferrets. The most well known is the National Ferret Welfare Society, which deals with all aspects of ferret keeping. There is also the Ferret Register, which aims to promote the traditional use of ferrets. Both organizations have links throughout the UK.
- Field sports suppliers that sell good-quality ferreting equipment such as purse nets and carrying boxes are usually able to help.

I recommend that you get your ferrets from someone who is truly enthusiastic about ferrets and has a working strain that dates back a number of years. Knowledge of its lineage will give you some idea of the makeup of the ferret you are buying – how it is likely to age and what its final size should be.

When not hunting, the ferret enjoys an active life.

Deciding Which Ferret to Buy

Knowing where to get a ferret is one thing, but how do you know if the ferret is healthy and has the makings of a good worker? To enable someone with no previous experience of ferrets to answer these questions, I have compiled the following guidelines.

The Ferret's Living Environment
Have a close look at the cages that the ferrets live in. They should be clean and fresh and this, in itself, is an indication of how well the animal is looked after. Dirty cages harbour parasites, increase the likelihood of foot rot and are definitely not the right conditions in which to raise kits. Nearly all the ferreters that I have met take a pride in the way they keep their ferrets, and these are the people it is best to buy a ferret from.

The Ferret's Appearance
You can tell a lot about a ferret's health by having a careful look at it and by handling it. The main features to note are shown below.

The coat should appear full with no sight of any thinning or bald patches. The coat of a healthy ferret has a lustre and body to it that is soft to the touch.

The eyes should be bright and possess an expression of life. Avoid any animals with eyes that appear sunken or recessed in their sockets. Although the eyes are lubricated by lacrimal fluid, there should not be any weeping of the eyes, evidenced by staining of the fur.

The teeth should be white and intact. You would not expect there to be any staining or tartar build-up in a young animal. Whilst inspecting the teeth you will be able to detect if there is any bad breath, which can be a warning of more serious problems such as abscesses and gum disease.

A healthy kit should have bright eyes and a keen expression.

The pads of the feet should be slightly pinkish in colour, with no redness, swelling or cracking. The claws should not be brittle, but strong and level with the base of the pad.

The feel of the ferret. Run your hand from the neck of the ferret down the full length of its body. Not only will this help you to assess the condition of the ferret's coat, you will also be able to feel any lumps or bumps on the body that need investigating. Bony prominences such as the ribs, shoulders and pelvis should have a cushion of flesh and muscle over them that prevents them from feeling hard. The hand of an adult should fit comfortably around the stomach of a young ferret and by so doing any bloating of the belly is quickly detected.

The Ferret's Activity

Observe the movement of the ferret, because this is the best indicator of the condition of the muscles and the bones of the skeleton to which they are attached. Movement should be fluid and coordinated, with all four paws making contact with the ground. Watch out for any swaying or weakness in the hindquarters.

The Ferret's Attitude

The ferret should be alert and show signs of interest in what is happening around it. Ferrets are, by nature, curious animals and will respond if you make a strange noise near them. The late Edward Ash, a renowned writer of dog books and a ferret keeper, recommended using the word 'puggy', with much accent placed on the 'pug' and 'gy' in order to attract the attention of the ferret. You can use a word of your own choosing, but bear in mind that the tone of voice is more important than the actual word. For example, I use 'chub-chub' as my ferret call. Do not feel self-conscious or silly when making such a sound.

27

When selecting kits, look for displays of normal behaviour such as playing with their siblings.

It is a very rudimentary way of communicating with a ferret, which will pay dividends later on when working the animal.

A young ferret of 10–12 weeks will probably not be completely tame and will still have an inclination to test strange things with its teeth. However, it should not be trying to bite everything in sight. When a ferret behaves like this, it is reasonable to assume that little time has been spent handling and socializing it as a kit. The ferret that you choose to buy should, at the very least, have some basic manners and show some signs of interest in, and enjoyment of, human company. Owing to its age, the ferret may struggle a little when being held, which is to be expected; it will do this by twirling the lower half of its body round and round.

A ferret that retreats to the corner of its cage or hisses at you when you try to get hold of it should be avoided. The former indicates that the ferret is scared and timid, and the latter is evidence of aggression. In ideal circumstances, the ferret that you choose should be active, observant and basically tame.

Now that you are able to recognize a healthy ferret, you can turn your attention to deciding whether to get an albino or a polecat, a hob or a jill, and how many of each.

Albino versus Polecat

These are the same animal and differ only in the colour of their coat and the colour of their eyes. Men who have hunted with ferrets for many decades state quite categorically that the colour of the ferret makes absolutely no difference to its working abilities. Both albinos and polecats make excellent hunters, and choosing between them is a matter of personal preference. There are suggestions that the albino is a slightly slower moving animal than the polecat due to its poorer eyesight. However, I have not noticed any lack of pace in the albinos that I have worked when there is the fresh scent of rabbit for them to follow, and it should be remembered that ferrets hunt primarily by scent. There are some situations that may favour a particular colour of ferret due to the fact that the coat will be more visible. For example, a polecat stands out more than an albino in the snow, whereas an albino is easier to see in areas thick with vegetation.

Hob versus Jill

Old books on ferreting reveal that jills were traditionally used for general rabbiting work, with the hobs being reserved for use as a line ferret, which, as the name implies, is a ferret that has a long line connected to its collar when it is entered to a warren. The intention was that it would locate and shift loose ferrets that were laid up below ground owing to a dead or trapped rabbit and, by means of the amount of line unravelled, the ferreter could determine where to start digging.

As a result of the popularity of locators, the line ferret has become virtually obsolete, which means that both hobs and jills are now worked loose within the warren; both are efficient hunters. One influential factor that should be considered when deciding between the two is the phenomenon known as sexual dimorphism, which results in the jills from a litter being smaller, shorter and possessing narrower bodies than their brothers. Therefore, the decision whether to have a hob or jill depends on whether you prefer a large or small working ferret.

I personally favour small ferrets for general rabbiting duties, and consequently the majority of my regular workers are jills. The reason for my preference is the ability of a small jill to pass through the mesh spaces of a set net without disturbing it, which means that they can exit and re-enter a warren under their own steam, with the ferreter only needing to keep an eye on them from a safe distance.

When I use the term 'small ferret', I am not referring to a specially bred minuscule version of a ferret, but simply to one that is at the smaller end of the naturally occurring scale of sizes for the species. The approximate measurement for such a ferret from the head to the base of the tail is between 11in and 12in (28cm and 30cm). When a hand is placed around its abdomen it should be possible to touch the tip of the third finger quite easily with the tip of the thumb. Small ferrets do have their critics, who claim that the little workers cannot endure being kicked by a large defensive rabbit and shirk their duties when faced with such confrontation. This has not been my experience, and I have found my little jills to be just as tough and determined when they are facing a rabbit as their bigger brethren would be.

In previous years I have hunted rabbits with some large hobs whose characters were as big as their bodies. They were both fun to use and able to make the rabbits bolt, although their work was not characterized by the same kind of finesse that the jills exhibit. They could not move through the nets and had a greater propensity for catching and killing rabbits in the warren, which was a distinct disadvantage. In spite of this, there are some working situations that favour the extra size and strength of the hob, such as under woodpiles where their ability to hold the rabbit can work to the ferreter's advantage. Admittedly, it is possible to acquire some small wiry

hobs that are not much bigger than a jill, and from a working perspective these can prove to be the equal of their female counterparts. However, they can be difficult to find. Ironically, the best working hob that I possess was rescued after being found in the coal bunker of a house in a nearby town.

When selecting a ferret, I recommend that you base your decision upon the size of the animal rather than its gender. If your intention is to choose the best potential worker, then select a small to medium animal, never a large one. Jills tend to conform to the best size for a working ferret with more regularity than the hobs and, as a result, a medium-sized jill will be the wisest purchase for a novice ferreter.

In the past, some people were put off keeping jills because it was believed that when a jill is left unmated, it becomes sick and dies. This is a hypothesis that ferreters continue to disagree about. Many respected ferreters have kept unmated jills, which have gone on to enjoy long and healthy lives despite never having kits. The majority of modern ferreters believe that a jill's prospects are limited if she is not mated or given an injection by the vet to bring her out of season.

You will be able to form your own opinion on this theory, but only after keeping ferrets for a few years. My jills have been left unmated and in season and have never suffered any health problems. When you consider the number of ferreters who have had the same experience, this cannot be explained as simply a matter of luck. At little expense or inconvenience, a ferret can be brought out of season by the vet, which is a perfect solution for those who do not wish to mate their jills but have concerns about their health.

How Many Ferrets are Needed?

The two main factors to consider when deciding how many ferrets you need are the size of the warrens where you will be hunting and whether you will be ferreting alone or in company. Traditional ferreters suggest that one ferret is required to work a small warren that has up to ten holes. Two ferrets are required for medium warrens with around twenty holes and three ferrets for large warrens of thirty or more holes.

However, bear in mind that if you are ferreting by yourself you should only deploy as many ferrets as you can comfortably watch over. One ferret is quite easy to keep an eye on, and I have found that two can also be easily managed by the single ferreter. I have entered three and sometimes four ferrets when hunting by myself, but it did get hectic at times and requires well-trained ferrets and open working environments. Therefore, if you intend to hunt by yourself, I advise that you do not take more than two ferrets. If you plan to hunt with a relative or friend, you may add two ferrets for each additional person until you have a maximum of six ferrets.

During twenty years of ferreting in a variety of locations, I have most commonly worked two ferrets in conjunction with a Jack Russell terrier. Even when faced with large, complicated warrens, two of my experienced ferrets were able to make quite an impression. It is possible to catch rabbits using only one ferret, and there are advantages to having only one working ferret – it will get plenty of use and, with regular use, it will become a better worker. I feel that it is better to have one ferret that gets plenty of opportunities to hunt than a large group, some of which rarely get the chance to come out of the carrying box. When I started ferreting I had two polecat jills, and I alternated using them on small warrens and doubled them up on the larger warrens. I think that two ferrets is an ideal number to start with. They will cope with most rabbit warrens and should be relatively easy to work while the ferreter learns his trade. When buying too many ferrets there is a danger that you will not have enough work for all of them. The only way to accurately determine how much work there will be for the ferrets is through practice. Therefore, I suggest that you complete a season's sport before acquiring more than two ferrets.

You should now have all the knowledge necessary to obtain a decent ferret for the purpose of hunting rabbits. We now turn our attention to other elements of the sport.

EQUIPMENT

Equipment for ferreting must perform well and be tough enough to endure being used in foul conditions and harsh environments by unsympathetic users. If an item is not well made, a few ferreting expeditions will highlight its weaknesses. There is nothing more frustrating than equipment that lets you down on the day of the hunt. Whether it is nets that malfunction, a spade that snaps in two like a twig when it is thrust into the ground, or a carrying box that separates from its strap when you are half a mile from home, they all test the resolve and patience of the ferreter and can be a real nuisance. However, by making some careful, well-informed choices, there is every chance of selecting equipment that will last for decades, if not a lifetime.

This traditional sport requires a minimum of equipment in order to succeed. A standard list of items will probably include the following:

- purse nets including net pegs
- carrying box or bag
- a digging tool/spade
- a knife
- a ferret finder, more commonly known as a locator
- a game bag/rucksack
- a flask
- a torch
- a first-aid kit
- appropriate clothing for the ferreter.

I shall now describe the construction and purpose of each of these.

Purse Nets

The purpose of a purse net is to cover every hole of a warren and catch the rabbit by tightening around it when the weight of its body hits the net.

The purse net is made from a piece of cord (*see* below) fashioned by a pattern of knots into a series of diamond shapes known as mesh spaces. A standard net is sixteen mesh spaces wide and eighteen mesh spaces long, resulting in an overall length of 36in (90cm). A purse net is bordered by drawcords of braided nylon, which are threaded through the mesh spaces at the edges of the net and connected to a peg, which is used to anchor the net to the ground. The net runs along these cords when they are pulled tight in response to a rabbit crashing into the net. The net then completely closes around the rabbit, creating what is known as the purse effect.

Purse nets are made from either hemp or nylon. Hemp is a natural material derived

A typical selection of ferreting equipment. 1, Light nylon line; 2, leather glove; 3, ferret bag; 4, handmade nets; 5, machine-made nets; 6, spade; 7, rogue bushman's hat; 8, Jack Russell (optional); 9, ripstop combat jacket; 10, German army moleskin trousers; 11, ferret carrying box; 12, transport box for car; 13, electronic ferret finders; 14, waterproof winter coat; 15, torch; 16, mallet; 17, binoculars; 18, game bag; 19, rucksack; 20, knives; 21, walking boots; 22, wellingtons; 23, first-aid kit.

from plants. It is graded according to its ply, which refers to the number of intertwined strands it possesses, which in turn determines the thickness of the hemp and thereby indicates its strength. An increase in the number corresponds to more strands and thicker hemp. Seven-ply hemp, which comprises seven strands of material, is considered to be the best thickness for rabbit purse nets.

Nylon is a man-made material. Its grading is indicated by a 'z', which denotes its breaking strain. Therefore, $4z$ refers to nylon with a breaking strain of 40lb (20kg) and $6z$ to a breaking strain of 60lb (30kg). The higher the breaking strain, the stronger the nylon will be. There are a variety of nylons, such as bonded nylon and smooth twisted nylon, which is used for machine-made nets. Spun nylon is ideal for making nets by hand owing to its softness. It produces nets of the highest quality, which have the best feel and are a pleasure to use.

Nets are available in a number of sizes: 3ft (90cm), 3½ft (100cm), 4ft (120cm) and

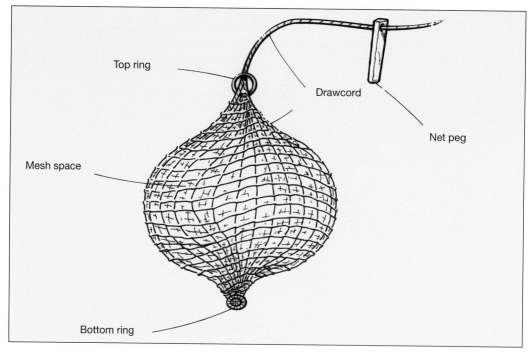

Top ring

Drawcord

Net peg

Mesh space

Bottom ring

The anatomy of a purse net.

5ft (150cm). Handmade nets can be any size you make them. Probably the most useful sizes are 3½ft (100cm) and 4ft (120cm), although some holes may require a larger net.

A good net should be easy to handle in all weather conditions, possess enough length so that it can cover different sized holes, be heavy enough to maintain its shape in windy conditions, and not become easily entangled when in use.

As already discussed, not all nets are the same. They can be long or short, straight or rounded, hemp or nylon, machine or handmade and cheap or expensive. Although some nets are definitely better than others, they are all capable of catching a rabbit. The cheapest nets are machine made and use thin nylon, which lacks the weight to hold its position when set, even in the slightest

breeze. They also tangle very easily, especially if you are not careful when pulling them out of the ground and wrapping them up. This does not mean that they cannot be used to catch rabbits, but the patience required to handle them soon puts the ferreter off wanting to use them on a regular basis.

Handmade nets are the most desirable. The net maker will use the best materials that are available, because good-quality materials make the task of constructing the net easier. Handmade nets are usually made by enthusiasts who take pride in what they produce. They can be expensive and cost considerably more than machine-made nets. However, they will last for many years and are therefore a good investment.

Some machine-made nets possess many of the qualities of handmade nets at a more affordable price. These are nylon nets of

A selection of purse nets. The net on the left is made by hand using spun nylon. Next to it are nets made of marine nylon, which are over 20 years old and still in good condition. The brightly coloured nets to the right are machine made.

10z. The increase in the 'z' factor means that they are thicker than entry-level nets and perform well in all types of weather conditions without becoming entangled.

The number of nets that you require depends on the size of the warrens where you intend to hunt. Look around the warrens and take note of approximately how many holes there are. Use this figure to work out the number of nets needed, bearing in mind that it is always worthwhile having a few extra nets so that you can quickly replace the nets into which the rabbits bolt. Most ferreters recommend a minimum of thirty nets to start with. I would not buy any more than this until they have been tested in the field.

In summary, I would advise that you purchase handmade nets of either 6z spun nylon or 7-ply hemp, or machine-made 10z nylon nets. There are businesses that specialize in supplying nets to ferreters, such as KP&S Nets, which was established 40 years

ago by Keith Pryer, a Dorset fisherman who swapped fishing nets for purse nets.

Net Pegs

Net pegs are used to anchor the net to the ground so that it will purse when the drawcords are pulled tight. They are commonly made of hardwood, have a hole in the upper part of the peg through which the drawcord is threaded and taper to a point at the opposite end of the peg. More recently they have been made with polypropylene and steel as used by campers. A standard net peg is 16–18cm long, 4cm wide at the top and 1.5cm wide at the bottom. They can be made longer if you ferret in an area where the soil structure is particularly loose. A good-quality peg should be easy to push into the ground, strong enough to be hit by a mallet if necessary and remain steadfast once it is in the ground.

A net wrapped up so that it can be easily packed in a game bag.

Most ferreters make their own pegs out of any scrap wood that is lying about. This is often pallet wood, and the pegs that are made from it are effective and long lasting. I made some of my first pegs from thick plywood, which is far from being the best type of wood to use but, rather surprisingly, I still have some of these pegs left after twenty years of use. One of the reasons why they have survived is that I covered them generously with paint prior to attaching them to the nets. This has helped to preserve them as well as making them more visible when it is time to collect the nets. Some traditional ferreters, who have access to woodlands, collect hazel, ash and blackthorn shanks, which they fashion into pegs once the wood is properly seasoned. The resulting pegs retain the cylindrical shape of the branch and have sharpened points akin to a spear or stake. The main disadvantage with these is that

it takes a minimum of one year for the wood to season.

Before I leave the subject of net pegs, I will mention the mallet, which is used to drive the pegs into hard ground. I did not include the mallet in the standard equipment list at the beginning of this section, because the majority of ferreters refuse to use a mallet. They believe that the noise generated when the head of the mallet strikes the top of the peg will be heard by, and deter, the rabbits from bolting. Ferreters who are willing to use a mallet are definitely in the minority, and I am one of them. For many years I have employed the mallet in the field when either the effects of the weather or the structure of the soil has made the ground impenetrable to a peg that is subject to hand pressure only. Because the mallet has a rubber striker, the noise it makes when it hits the peg is kept to a minimum. In my experience, it has not been responsible for rabbits failing to bolt from the warren. Sometimes we can be overcautious about alerting rabbits, which are, in the vast majority of cases, accustomed to the noises of modern life, particularly the banging and clattering of farm machinery.

Admittedly, the mallet will only be needed occasionally, but I have no hesitation in using it. For me, the correct securing of the net is worth the annoyance of some intermittent muffled noise. If you regularly encounter hard ground or have trouble pushing net pegs in, a mallet is worth trying.

Carrying Box

A carrying box is used to transport ferrets during a day's rabbiting. It is usually rectangular in shape with an opening lid on the top and air vents at either the side or the front. Carrying boxes are made of lightweight wood such as thin plywood or 9mm OSB strandboard. Their size varies depending upon the number of ferrets that are to be carried. Approximate measurements for a carrying box suitable for one large or two small ferrets are length 30cm, height 20cm and width 15cm. For two medium-sized ferrets or three small

A sturdy homemade carrying box.

ones the minimum dimensions for a carrying box are length 35cm, height 25cm and width 25cm.

A good carrying box should be easy to open, comfortable to carry and not too heavy. It is the most popular way of transporting ferrets, because it provides a safe, solid and secure environment for them as well as offering satisfactory protection from all types of weather. They are quite easy to make and, with the added protection of a suitable preservative, will last for decades.

Carrying Bag

The carrying bag, or carry bag, performs the same task as the carrying box – the safe transportation of the ferret from one warren to another during a day's rabbiting.

The ferret carry bag is a lightweight alternative to the carrying box.

The ferret is happy to be transported in a bag that is used correctly.

It is an open-top sack with brass rings spaced along the top through which a nylon cord is threaded, which when pulled tight will shut the bag. The bag also has breather holes at the front and back for the ferret.

Modern bags are made of heavy-duty canvas. They are available as a single, which carry one ferret, or a double, which has the capacity to hold two ferrets. The bag must be well sewn together and made of premium-grade canvas in order to give it the necessary toughness to contain and transport the ferret.

During the course of my ferreting I have made use of both boxes and bags and, in my opinion, bags have a number of advantages over boxes: they are lighter, smaller and easier to carry owing to their shape. They are also more versatile than boxes and can be carried in a variety of ways. For instance, a strap can be attached to them so that they can be carried over the shoulder like a game bag or, alternatively, they may be placed in the top of a rucksack on top of the nets. A bag offers the ferret more freedom of movement than the average box. This is because the structure of the bag is flexible instead of solid, and when it is tied correctly the bag forms a comfortable dome shape around the ferret. Contrary to what many people think, the ferret is quite secure within the bag and is not thrown about when the ferreter is on the move. In fact, the ferret is as comfortably held as it would be in a box.

Most modern ferreters use carrying boxes in favour of bags. However, photographs of ferreters during the early 1900s show that they regularly used bags to carry their ferrets. I was dismissive of bags until I actually tried one, and to my surprise I found that I preferred using them to carrying boxes. I also learnt that many of the criticisms levelled at them are unwarranted.

The bag is a comfortable and convenient way to carry a ferret. My ferrets have shown no objections to them and emerge fresh, clean, content and ready for work when the bag is opened. The only downside is that you will need more than one bag if you want either to take more than two ferrets or to carry two ferrets separately. However, the lightness of the bags means that this is not difficult.

Digging Tool/Spade

A digging tool is needed to cut narrow holes into the ground so that a tunnel can be formed linking into the warren. The ferreter can place his arm through this tunnel to retrieve a ferret that has a rabbit cornered, a live rabbit or a rabbit that has been killed below ground.

The ideal rabbiter's spade has a long narrow head attached to a strong shaft. The shaft may be made of either wood, metal, plastic or fibreglass. The head is metal. The handle may be as short as 48cm for use on steep banks where a knee can be leant on the bank to help maintain balance.

For general work the spade is of medium size and has a handle measuring 67cm. With the head this gives an overall length of 105cm.

In open space where deep holes are required, a long spade is needed. The handle for one of these should be at least 105cm long. Long spades are also valuable amongst rocky ground because the length of the handle means that the spade can be used as an effective lever to move a heavy rock.

A selection of spades enables the ferreter to dig into the warren and tidy the ground when the dig is finished.

The most commonly used spades. From the left: a long-handled spade used for digging deep holes; a lightweight spade for general digging duties; a short-handled spade that is ideal when digging on a slope.

The narrow head should remain more or less the same size for all three types of spade. The dimensions for a suitable spade head are around 26cm long and 10cm+ wide. The ideal ferreter's spade should be light to carry and very strong. The spade is one of the ferreter's most important tools. He should have one of good quality that is suited to the task of digging into warrens.

General gardening spades have a broader head than is necessary, which will result in more earth than is required being moved. The best type of spade for the ferreter is found amongst those categorized as drain spades. An excellent example is the Newcastle Drainer, which is specifically designed for digging deep narrow holes. I, like many ferreters, have collected a number of spades over many years and some of them are more suitable for use in certain environments than others. For example, I have a long-handled all-metal spade that is always used when the ground is covered with rocks. It may be heavy, but it is also indestructible and can be driven into the hardest ground reasonably easily. For general duties I have a standard draining spade, which I find easy to carry as the handle fits neatly through the leather straps of my roe sack. This spade has a fibreglass shaft, which means that it is incredibly light and can be carried all day with ease.

Knife

A knife is used principally for legging rabbits in the field so that they may be carried easily (see page 86). A knife is also needed to gut, skin and joint the rabbit so that it can either be stored in the freezer or cooked. I always leave the task of gutting and skinning the rabbit until I get home, where I have an assortment of skinning and butchering knives. However, because the rabbit is small game, it is possible to perform all field and butchery tasks with just one knife. This is perfectly illustrated by American hunter Sam Fadala, who skins and joints rabbits in the field so that he can carry the meat home in freezer bags

placed in a rucksack. He uses a Puma lock knife, and claims that this only takes him a few minutes.

There are three types of knife available for the ferreter to choose from:

1. **One-piece or sheath knife**. This is selected for its strength and because it is easy to use. There is no need to open and shut the blade every time you want to use it. Only having to withdraw the knife from its sheath is ideal for the ferreter in winter weather when he has cold or wet fingertips.

2. **Lock knife**. This is a folding knife with a lockback mechanism that is designed to hold the blade fixed in position when it is open. Although this undeniably gives the knife strength, its main intention is to prevent the blade accidentally closing on the

A good knife enables the ferreter to leg the rabbits so that they can be handled easily. The rope is used to tie the rabbits together so that they can be carried over the ferreter's shoulder.

fingers when it is subjected to pressure. This safety measure makes it a popular choice amongst all hunters.

3. **Folding knife**. This is the traditional penknife, which typically has a smaller blade than the lock knife and lacks any form of locking mechanism. The combination of these factors means that this type of knife is often overlooked as a hunting tool. However, there are plenty of good examples available today that can be used to leg and even skin a rabbit, and they are worthy of a place in the ferreter's kit.

Knife handles are most commonly made of wood, lightweight metal, antlers or rubber. The majority of blades are made of either carbon or stainless steel. Companies such as Buck Knives of America use high-quality steels with alloy blends for their blades and all the metal is heat-treated. This is a process that involves heating, freezing and then reheating the metal. The resulting blades possess strength, good corrosion and wear resistance as well as edge retention and resharpenability. Always choose a knife with a blade that is ideally suited for fieldwork on a rabbit. Buck produces knives specifically for use on small game; the blades start at 6.5cm and do not exceed 10cm. A large blade is not necessary for dealing with a rabbit.

This small Buck Solo folding knife has proven to be an excellent tool for legging rabbits in the field and, despite not having a lock, the blade has never moved from its open position when in use.

This Buck Protege lock knife is intended for outdoor use and, as such, provides the ferreter with a handle that is easy to hold on to when his hands are wet and cold.

This Buck Caping knife was designed for intricate cutting work and is ideal when skinning and jointing small game such as rabbits.

The ferreter's knife should be comfortable to grip in all types of weather and when hands are wet, covered with mud or slippery. It should be easy to open if it is a folding or lock knife. I have a knife with a blade perfectly shaped for legging rabbits, but I can only open it with my teeth or a pair of pliers. The former is highly dangerous while the latter is impractical, which means the knife is useless. The knife should possess good edge retention so that it remains sharp even after legging many rabbits. It should be resistant to rust so that it can be used in wet conditions and, after a day's work, be immersed in a bucket of hot water in order to clean it thoroughly. Finally, it should be light to carry whether worn in a pouch that slides on a belt or carried in a pocket.

The knife is unique amongst the ferreter's kit because there are laws that govern where it can be carried and how it should be used. Therefore, the ferreter, like every other knife user, needs to be aware of current legislation and demonstrate an unhesitating willingness to comply with it. Basically, the law at present states that the ferreter can only carry a sheath knife, lock knife or a folding knife with a blade exceeding 3in (5cm) when there is a legitimate task for the knife to perform, such as legging rabbits. The carrying of the knife should be confined to the environment where this job is undertaken. To carry any of these knives when you are not hunting and have no work for them to do is a legal offence.

Together with an awareness of the law, a knife user should appreciate how members of the public feel about knives. Consequently, I think carefully about which knives to use when I am ferreting and in which location I should use a particular type of knife. This is so that I can both abide by the law and avoid offending anyone.

When ferreting at a site where members of the public are likely to be passing by,

43

such as on a golf course or near a footpath, I use a Buck Solo folding knife that has a blade measuring 6.5cm. Despite its size, the blade is razor sharp and ideally suited to cutting through the flesh of the rabbit so that it can be legged and gutted. There are no legal restrictions relating to the carrying of a knife this size that has no locking mechanism, and it is very unlikely that any member of the public would feel threatened by the appearance of this knife.

When I am ferreting on more remote, or private, ground, where I am unlikely to encounter people and where most of my ferreting takes place, I use a Buck Protege 3in lockback knife. This is from their outdoor range and, as well as being amazingly light, has the best handle to grip when working in the field.

For the purpose of gutting, skinning and jointing the rabbit, which I always leave until I get home, I use a Buck Caping knife, which is a sheath knife with a 9cm blade. Chad Schearer of Montana, who is a World Champion Elk Caller, designed this knife, and it boasts a unique blade shape ideal for intricate cutting strokes. As a result it makes short work of butchering small game, including rabbits, and it is easy to clean once the job is finished.

As a final comment on knives for ferreting, I suggest that you select a knife made

Many ferreters hold the opinion that locators are an essential piece of equipment. In the right hands they can be very useful.

In conjunction with a locator, a transmitter is fitted to a collar worn by the working ferret.

by a company that specializes in hunting and outdoor knives so that if you are ever challenged you can point out that you are using the bona fide tool for the job.

Ferret Finder

The ferret finder, commonly referred to as a locator, is used to pin-point the whereabouts of a ferret when it is in the warren. It can monitor the progress of the ferret and detect when it has become stationary, either because a rabbit has been cornered or killed. By so doing the locator provides the ferreter with the precise position to start digging.

The ferret finder consists of two pieces of equipment. The first is the transmitter, which is contained within a small rectangular box that slides on to a 200mm collar and fastens around the ferret's neck. The second part of the ferret finder is the receiver, which is a plastic box measuring 16cm × 7cm and weighing 186g when the battery is inserted. The transmitter emits a signal that the receiver picks up and broadcasts as audible bleeps or pips. The closer the ferreter moves to the transmitter, the higher the pitch of the bleeps becomes. When the pitch is at its highest the ferreter should be above his animal. The receiver operates as far away from the transmitter as 16ft (5m) and an LED display shows the distance that is between the two.

Modern ferret finders cost around £150. In defence of this price it is worth pointing out that they are reliable, reduce the chance of losing a ferret, and make digging more accurate and consequently less time-consuming.

Some practice is required before you are fully *au fait* with them. If possible, I recommend that you use someone else's before purchasing one.

Some ferreters claim that the locator is an essential piece of equipment that no ferreter should be without. I do not agree. Locators undeniably offer benefits, but ferreters did manage for centuries before the locator was invented and some, albeit a minority, continue to do so. I have been using ferrets to catch rabbits for over twenty years and I have never used a locator.

Game Bag/Rucksack

The game bag, or rucksack, is used to carry purse nets and all the other pieces of equipment that the ferreter requires during a day's rabbiting. A good bag must be comfortable to carry, extremely tough, weather resistant, preferably waterproof and easy to access.

Game bags come in a variety of sizes, but the most common size is approximately 40cm from end to end and 30cm high. A traditional game bag is made of cotton canvas and has a lift-over flap with leather ties.

An assortment of bags for carrying the equipment needed for a day's ferreting. On the left is a tough traditional game bag made by Jack Pyke. In the centre is a rucksack, which is a comfortable alternative to game bags, and on the right is a roe sack that incorporates a removable waterproof liner.

They are usually green in colour and may have two front compartments or a mesh front pouch that is the length of the bag. Jack Pyke of England are using a material called duotex to make their game bags. This is relatively new on the market and is proving to be both tough and durable.

A number of ferreters opt for a rucksack as an alternative to the traditional game bag, and for good reason. Most notably the rucksack has two straps, which means that the burden is borne jointly by the large muscles of the shoulders and back. Modern rucksacks are extremely comfortable and have a number of useful compartments, which enable the ferreter to divide his equipment conveniently, with the most-used items such as the nets occupying the large central compartment. The rucksack is probably the best way to carry loads over long distances and difficult terrain, which is why armies from all over the world use them. Similar to a rucksack is the roe sack, which, as its name suggests, has been designed for deerstalkers, but this does not prevent it from being of use to the ferreter. Roe sacks are similar to the rucksacks of 50 years ago owing to the leather shoulder straps and simple hook attachment. My roe sack has a voluminous central compartment and three front pockets. Although it cost more than a rucksack, it is built to last and has a larger carrying capacity. The roe sack is ideal when I am only after a couple of rabbits because it has been designed to carry game. Consequently, the dead rabbits and all the equipment can be carried in the same bag.

The choice between game bag, rucksack or roe sack is a matter of personal preference. All of them are equally suitable for the ferreter's purpose. None of them need cost a fortune and they will offer decades, if not a lifetime, of service.

Flask

This is probably one of the most appreciated items that the ferreter carries. After standing on a hillside, buffeted by unrelenting wind, or walking miles and undertaking numerous tiring digs, a warm drink is a welcome treat. When selecting a flask choose an all-metal one that is indestructible.

As well as a flask, I carry a lightweight aluminium drink bottle that is filled with water for the dogs and ferrets. I have a 400ml bottle for outings of short duration and an 800ml bottle for a full day in the field.

Ferreting can be thirsty work and a flask containing a warm drink is always appreciated.

The other members of the ferreting team are also in need of regular refreshment, and tough, lightweight water bottles are ideal for this.

Torch

A torch is used to help illuminate dark areas. This is particularly useful when working ferrets around old farm buildings and often during the course of a dig. When digging into the warren the torchlight enables the ferreter to identify the rabbit and ferret quicker than he would be able to with just the naked eye.

A lightweight low-energy torch should suffice for the ferreter's purposes. There are plenty of good torches available that are not much bigger than a pen and so fit easily into a pocket or on to a belt. A headlamp can also be used. This need not be hand-held and is particularly useful when the ferreter has to retrieve his ferret from a dark tunnel or wants to dig or move obstacles out of the way. There are also torches available that do not require batteries. They operate by either shaking or winding.

First-Aid Kit

A first-aid kit can be used to treat minor injuries in a safe and appropriate way. It should contain an antiseptic cleansing wipe or normal saline to cleanse a wound, a wound pad or waterproof plasters to dress the wound, and a bandage and surgical tape to hold the dressing in place.

In my experience, the most common injuries to afflict the ferreter are minor cuts and bruises. Barbed wire and the briers of hedges, such as blackthorn, cause the majority of cuts. The hands are the most common sites of injury. Most hand injuries occur when reaching into the hedge to set nets. Ferreter's legs are usually well protected by wax leggings. However, straddling barbed wire fences is risky. All injuries should be dealt with immediately. A break in the skin should be cleaned and dressed with a bandage or plaster. Not only

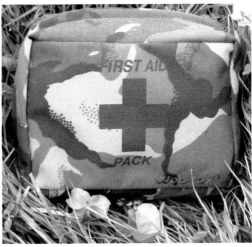

In some situations, torch light is a great help to the ferreter. Both these torches also allow the ferreter to keep his hands free.

A small first-aid kit takes up little room and is always worth carrying.

will this enable the ferreter to continue with his day's sport in more comfort, it will also reduce the risk of infection and need for further treatment.

The minor first-aid kit occupies little space in the game bag, and it will also come in useful if either a ferret or dog is injured. Considering some of the remote locations that the ferreter hunts at, it is a good idea to carry one. The ferreter, and others who spend a lot of time outdoors in isolated places, should consider the benefits of attending a first-aid course.

Clothing

Clothing should provide the ferreter with protection from the weather and, to some extent, from injuries that can be caused by barbed wire or prickly hedges.

It is possible to ferret through the winter despite wind, rain, hail, frost or snow. The combination of bad weather and exposed locations that ferreters may encounter in the hill country of Wales, England, Scotland and Ireland makes appropriate clothing vital. In the past, people who lived and worked outside, such as the rabbit trappers of Pembrokeshire, the hill shepherds of Cumbria, the farm labourers of Lancashire and the crofters of Caithness, understood the importance of clothing and were very particular about their requirements. The nature of ferreting also necessitates a wise choice of clothing, because there will be periods of time when the ferreter has to remain still, even on the coldest of days. Another factor to consider is the weather that most typifies the county in which you live or hunt. As a general rule, the further north you go the colder it gets and the further west the wetter it becomes.

Over the past twenty years I have worn an assortment of clothes for ferreting. These include waxproof coats and leggings, but I have also been known to set out for a day's sport wearing a pure wool overcoat, and

I once tried a pair of hobnail boots. Some of the clothes quickly became favourites, while others proved to be totally useless for my purpose. Generally speaking, the items that are selected should possess the following characteristics:

- They should be made of material that is tough and durable and will not rip easily.
- Both footwear and clothing should be 100 per cent waterproof.
- The clothing must be well tailored so that it provides room for movement when the ferreter is digging or bending down to set nets.
- Coats and trousers should have a number of usable pockets.

My list of clothing for ferreting, which is used year after year, includes the following items. Wellington boots are ideal for muddy conditions or if you have to net and guard a warren positioned on the slope of a ditch that has water in the bottom. Walking or hunting boots are the best choice if long distances or precarious ground are to be covered. My favourite boots are modelled on the moccasins worn by Native Americans. They are light, totally waterproof and they bend effortlessly with the foot when kneeling to set nets.

Army surplus or military-style trousers are the best type of trousers because they have plenty of pockets, two of which are large cargo pockets that are ideal for carrying a dog lead and slipping a couple of nets into. I also wear leggings, which perform three functions: they keep me dry and warm in wet, windy weather; they protect my trousers and legs from barbed wire and stinging nettles; and they enable me to kneel on sodden ground when setting nets. I favour waxed cotton leggings because they are virtually indestructible.

I need comfortable footwear for ferreting. A boot has to be light, 100 per cent waterproof and supple enough to conform to the contours of the foot when bending or kneeling to set nets.

I have a lightweight waterproof coat for those days when it is pouring with rain and reasonably warm. An army surplus Gore-Tex parka with no lining is ideal. My main winter coat has to be able to withstand the worst winter weather. I have two such coats so that one can be worn while the other is being dried.

My grandfather used to say that a man should never leave the house without a hat on his head. In his day it was a choice between a trilby hat and a flat cap, but nowadays there are many more varieties to choose from. A hat will keep your head dry and prevent heat loss on bitterly cold days.

I use fingerless gloves because they do not get in the way or need removing when I am dealing with nets. Leather is the best material for these since wool is too easily caught and pulled on sharp objects.

With an army surplus Gore-Tex parka, a pair of wax leggings and a leather bushman's hat, I am ideally dressed for wet days.

Fingerless gloves are useful because they provide protection from the cold but do not get in the way of handling nets. I am also wearing a lined Dutch army parka that has kept me warm during the notorious Scottish winters.

51

The Walking Stick

Today we tend to associate sticks in general and walking sticks in particular with the aged and infirm, but it is only half a century ago that countrymen, especially hill shepherds and gamekeepers, employed walking sticks in their everyday life. They used their sticks to help combat fatigue and provide secure footing as they walked over many miles of steep and precarious land. In boggy ground or marshes, the walking stick was used as a probe to find a safe path.

American hunters still use sticks, and Sam Fadala, author of *Game Care and Cookery*, affectionately refers to his as the Moses stick. He states quite emphatically that he would not be happy if he went hunting without it.

When my father presented me with a walking stick on my birthday many years ago, I was obliged to try and find a use for it, particularly when I discovered that he had spent many hours fashioning it from a crude branch into an elegant three-quarter-length thumb stick. Although I was reluctant to take it along to start with, I soon discovered that it could perform a number of useful tasks during the course of a day's ferreting. I shall briefly describe the uses of the walking stick in the hope of reviving interest in this forgotten tool.

Using a walking stick to take nets from one warren to another.

A walking stick can aid the ferreter over rough ground and is ideally suited for poking about in undergrowth and hedges in the search for bolt holes. If the stick is of a decent length, it can be driven into the ground to make a secure stand for hanging coats, hats, carrying boxes or a rabbit. When an equal number of dead rabbits are slipped over each end of the stick and it is held in the middle, it becomes a simple and convenient rabbit transporter.

There are many types of walking stick available, for example the one-piece stick, leg cleek, crook, knob stick and thumb stick. I strongly recommend the thumb stick because it is capped with a V shape, which is ideal for slipping the rings of the purse nets onto. Consequently, the thumb stick can be used to carry nets between warrens that lie within close proximity to one another without having to fold them up and unravel them again soon after. The rings of the net are slipped over either side of the V shape, and the stick can be carried with its base in one hand and the upper portion of the stick resting on the shoulder so that the purse nets hang straight down the back. The stick is held in the same way that a rifle is carried by a soldier on parade. I have done this numerous times with as many as twenty nets hanging from my thumb stick, and they have never got tangled. Using a stick in this way makes the setting and gathering of nets much

Using a walking stick to transport rabbits.

easier and quicker when working a number of warrens that lie within a relatively short distance of one another. A walking stick does not add to your load but helps you to deal with your burden, hence it was said that the professional hill dweller would never think of leaving his house without his stick.

DOGS FOR FERRETING

A good ferreting dog is worth its weight in gold and will not only help the field sportsman achieve success when out hunting, but will increase the level of enjoyment of each day spent working ferrets. Both terrier and ferret have enjoyed such a long association within the sport that a terrier seems to be the obvious choice of dog for the ferreter.

However, we would be wrong to think that the terrier is the only dog that can be used to good effect when ferreting. A survey of rural photographs appearing in *The Field* magazine and other similar publications during the first half of the 20th century support this view. They show a great variety of dogs partnered with ferrets and in pursuit of rabbits. Most of these dogs are unstandardized and widely dissimilar, lacking conformity in either size or appearance. Any attempt to determine their lineage would be pure guesswork. This is hardly surprising because, as Ivester Lloyd points out, 'next to fishing the most popular sport of countrymen and boys used to be had from watching a dog as it hunts rabbits.' More often than not the family dog sufficed.

There are numerous tales told by elderly countrymen about their first experiences of field sports, during which they made use of some quite unlikely and seemingly unsuitable dogs for the activity that they were performing. To many of us the majority of these dogs would appear to be mongrels, but their owners euphemistically claimed that they were cottager's dogs. Although Britain boasts an unrivalled reputation for developing breeds for a specific task or purpose, my grandfather and many of his contemporaries espoused the idea that if you kept a dog it should be able to do any job asked of it. In return the dog would enjoy a good home, good food and plenty of stimulating activity. My grandfather possessed genuine affection for his dogs, but this was tempered by the belief that a dog should earn its keep. Consequently, the country dog was expected to be a jack-of-all-trades, which meant that there were many mediocre rabbiting dogs about at the time.

The inadequacies of such dogs were tolerated, if not ignored, and one has to remember that, with the countryside seemingly overrun with rabbits, the pursuit of coney was far easier and much less frustrating than many people find it today. Admittedly, the keenest of rabbiters and professional warreners alike would always choose a member of the terrier or sighthound group because such dogs possessed the best reputation for hunting rabbits.

With the coming of myxomatosis, changes in farming and loss of warren sites, catching rabbits became more difficult and less rewarding. The 'any dog will do' philosophy was quickly abandoned and, like the warreners of old, the ferreter now wanted a terrier, small lurcher or Whippet. These are still the most popular hunting dogs today. Among my own acquaintances, terriers are by far the most common working dog used with ferrets, in particular small terriers of 11in (28cm) in height and less. My brother is of the opinion that for ratting and rabbiting the smaller the terrier the better. He is supported in his belief by the writing of Dan Russell, who speaks of terriers as small as 4lb (2kg) or 5lb (2.5kg) being capital ratters and who recommends Yorkshire and Norwich terriers. He states in his book, *Working Terriers*, that 'it is an amazing sight to see a little Yorkshire tackle and kill a rat almost as big as itself.' He also mentions a gentleman who bred Yorkshire terriers especially for hunting rabbits. Other choice breeds for ferreters include the Cairn, Norfolk, Australian and Jack Russell terriers. Obviously the larger, heavier terriers can and will catch rabbits, but they are neither as handy nor as proficient as their smaller cousins.

There are numerous reasons why these small terriers make such good ferreting dogs. They possess a keen hunting instinct and a natural talent for the work. In the words of Dan Russell, 'there is a distinctive style and smartness about the way in which a well broken, keen terrier does the job which other dogs do not possess.' Although he is speaking about ratting, the same is true when using the terrier for rabbiting. Terriers are anatomically suited to work around the warren. Their size enables them to move quickly in confined spaces and through the densest undergrowth. The smallest of terriers will take on the biggest of challenges and they are unequalled in their ability to penetrate

A terrier is a perfect companion for any ferreter and cannot be bettered in regard to working at a warren.

deep cover. An 11in (30cm) terrier can penetrate cover that a burly man wearing thornproof leggings and coat cannot push through.

Terriers are decisive and quick with their jaws. They appear to possess an instinctive understanding of subterranean activity and are accurate indicators of rabbit movement below ground. They also have an alertness bordering on nosiness, which prevents them missing any important activity. Generally, they work well with other dogs and are not difficult to socialize with livestock. They have a hardy constitution, which makes them suitable for winter work. Finally, they are easy to come by and not too expensive, particularly the smaller Jack Russell types for which a large gene pool of working stock is available.

Whippets are also a favourite with rabbiters. They are preferred to larger sighthounds because they reach full speed more quickly and show greater balance on sharp turns. The Whippet was bred for catching rabbits, although not in the most sporting of circumstances. It is tailor made to pursue a fleeing rabbit as it makes a short, sharp dash from one warren to another. It is also a suitable size for close work at the warren. Terrier enthusiasts will doubtless claim that such usefulness is derived from the infusion of terrier blood during the Whippet's early history. There are some doubts about its ability to endure the worst of the winter weather, despite devotees claiming that the Whippet is not as fragile as it looks.

It cannot be denied that the Whippet is a good rabbiter and has an excellent temperament. Nevertheless, some people are opting for the best of both worlds by using small lurchers that combine the qualities of both the Whippet and the terrier and have more enduring hardiness than the former and greater speed than the latter.

In conclusion, throughout history a wide variety of dogs have been used for ferreting with varying degrees of success. However, the terrier and the Whippet have proved themselves to be the best dogs for the ferreter.

WHERE TO LOOK FOR RABBITS AND HOW TO GET PERMISSION TO HUNT

In order to ferret you will need access to land inhabited by a decent population of rabbits. Securing permission to go on such land is arguably one of the most difficult aspects of the sport, because it is reliant upon the beneficence of another person and, apart from making a good impression, is largely out of the ferreter's hands. Finding good hunting sites and acquiring permission to go on them is as vital to the success of ferreting as such skills as setting nets.

The process of gaining permission to rabbit is not the most exciting aspect of ferreting and some will find it tedious. However, ferreters are compelled legally and ethically to gain permission from landowners before they hunt. The only exception to this rule is if you are in possession of your own land, i.e. if you are a farmer or smallholder. Barring this exception there is no land that you have the right to hunt on without prior consent. Even common ground falls under the authority of nearby residents who possess old agreements granting them grazing rights. Legally, all the ferreter requires is the consent of the landowner or, in the case of public schools, golf courses or land belonging to the council, the agreement of

Agricultural land has proved to be the most common ground that I have found rabbits on, particularly when it is bordered by neglected areas such as this derelict steading.

an authorized person such as a grounds-man or caretaker.

When I started ferreting many years ago, I was granted access to all the land I hunted by verbal agreement. However, times have changed and the modern ferreter now seeks the safeguard of written permission. This need not be complicated; an outline of what the ferreter can do and where and when he can do it should suffice. A letter containing these details can be presented for the landowner to sign. When hunting on land belonging to the local authority, which falls under the public gaze, I suggest

---

Questions to Ask a Landowner when Acquiring Permission to Ferret

- Are there any particular days and times when you can or cannot visit the ground?
- Is it acceptable to use dogs in conjunction with the ferrets?
- Are there any restricted areas on the ground where the ferreter is not to go?
- Are there any hazards that the ferreter should be made aware of or avoid, i.e. potentially dangerous livestock or tractor crossings?
- Is it acceptable to dig when necessary?
- Is the ferreter allowed to clear any vegetation around the warren that is restricting his access to the holes?
- When appropriate, can a four-wheel-drive vehicle be taken on the ground?

---

taking the added precaution of having the contact number of an authorized person to refer to in the unlikely event that you are ever challenged.

Finding land that is worth acquiring access to may require patience and determination but, in the ferreter's favour, the rabbit is found throughout the UK and the damage they cause when high in numbers means that many people want them controlled. So how does the ferreter find some land? There are a number of options, which are outlined below.

If you live in the countryside, this is the best place to start. You are likely to be personally acquainted with the landowner or know somebody who is, and the fact that you are looking for good

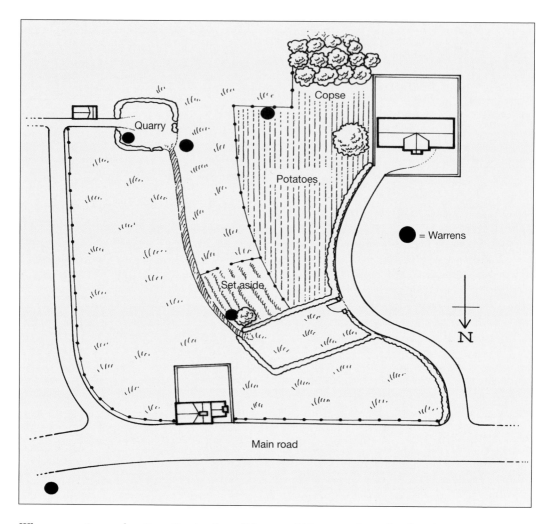

When access to new hunting sites is given, it is a good idea to make a simple reference map showing the location of warrens.

ferreting ground will spread by word of mouth in small communities. Also, you will have local knowledge of the landscape and will be able to see where and in what numbers the rabbits are appearing. For me, one of the benefits of local ferreting is the short distance involved in travelling to the site. When I have had to resort to using the car, I have been able to get to the vast majority of warrens within twenty minutes. I am fortunate enough to have a number of good warrens, which can sustain a season's hunting, within walking distance of my home. During the course of my reading I have noted that during the 1940s and 1950s ferreters mostly travelled either by foot or bicycle, and for the younger ferreter of today such methods of transport remain the most useful.

As already mentioned, you can rely on word of mouth in a small community to let people know you are looking for hunting ground. If you want to speed up the process or extend your area of activity, you can either visit likely looking farms or leave a leaflet or card advertising your services in a place that farmers regularly frequent, such as agricultural suppliers, feed merchants, farmers' co-operatives and saddlers. If you choose to call on farmers without prior introduction, it is vital that you make the right impression. Therefore, I strongly recommend that you confine your visits to daylight hours, do not turn up clad in camouflage from head to toe, and do offer a full and frank explanation of what ferreting with purse nets entails. Following the outbreaks of foot-and-mouth disease and with the concerns about avian flu, the majority of farms have stringent biosecurity measures; these must be respected when visiting any farms.

If you are willing to travel considerable distances, land may be acquired via advertisements placed in either farming or field sports periodicals. Letters of enquiry concerning rabbit damage and the need for control may be sent to such amenities as golf clubs and riding stables.

The ferreter can secure access to land by turning professional and establishing a pest control business. He will then have both the time and financial reward to survey a much larger area than the weekend ferreter, but the demands for success will be much greater.

In conclusion, it takes time and patience to acquire ground where the rabbits are plentiful. When acquiring rabbiting rights, an intimate knowledge of the area and an ear well pressed to the ground will pay dividends. It is an aspect of ferreting that could not be described as exciting, but we have met some interesting characters in our endeavours to acquire permission to access land. Do not be reluctant or embarrassed to ask permission, because the worst a person can do is refuse, which is the landowner's privilege.

GETTING THE FERRETS READY FOR HUNTING

The hunting of rabbits in a warren is physically challenging for the working ferret and, like the marathon runner, the ferret will need some form of training to ensure that it is ready for this work. This training concentrates on developing physical fitness, encouraging correct behaviour and providing the ferret with some working savvy. Exercise, regular handling and exposure to nets and warrens are all part of the ferret's training. Consequently, the items employed during training are a secure exercise run, collar and long lead, some drainpipes and a practice warren.

A polecat ferret climbing over logs that have been placed in its exercise run. This helps develop stamina and adeptness for moving over and through some of the obstacles it is likely to encounter when hunting.

The Training Schedule

This involves 30min per day in the exercise run with the ferreter, which will help develop the strength and stamina of the ferret. The athleticism of the ferret and its capacity for exercise are often overlooked. My ferrets have shown by practical demonstration that they can climb, swim, run at speed, jump, squeeze through tight apertures, drag weights far in excess of their own size and grip with their teeth for dear life. In the world of athletics, the ferret could justly be compared to the decathlete who possesses the talent to excel at numerous disciplines.

Whilst in the exercise run the ferret should be picked up regularly, held for a

A ferret should be alert, in good condition and attentive to the handler if it is going to be used for rabbiting.

Moving through hollowed-out logs and drain pipes helps to condition the ferret and prepare it for movement through a warren.

short time and then released. Once the ferret is used to being picked up, put the drainage pipes in the run. The ferret can then be picked up as it comes out of the pipe. This will serve as a crude simulation of picking up a ferret when it exits a warren and will go some way to preventing such transgressions as skulking.

The schedule should also include 20min lead walking every other day. The ferret, although built on very small legs, can walk considerable distances. Lead walking is a good way of enabling it to do this in new environments that offer added stimulation. The ferreter should occasionally stop and pick the ferret up so that it becomes used to being handled in unfamiliar surroundings.

Loose exercise (10–20min) twice a week is also part of the training schedule. Ferrets love the freedom of unrestrained movement and being able to move beyond the confines of a cage or run. This type of exercise should be closely supervised. You will sometimes need to redirect the ferret so that it remains in a safe area, such as on the lawn in your back garden. Most ferrets get excited during this form of exercise and picking it up will be a good test of its temperament.

When the ferret is 100 per cent tame and reliable to handle, it can be taken once a week to a practice warren. This can be a redundant warren where there is no incentive of fresh rabbit scent to prompt the ferret. Hopefully, the ferret's natural

curiosity will take it through the warren. Do not be worried if the ferret does not go deep in to the warren. After a couple of times through the warren, a net can be placed over some of the holes so that the ferret develops some rudimentary net sense. I avoid overdoing my ferret at the practice warren because I do not want it to get bored or lose interest. If you do not have a suitable practice warren within easy distance of home, you could build a simple one in the corner of your back garden.

The Results of the Training Schedule

After putting a ferret through a training schedule such as the one described above it will be as fit as it possibly can be and therefore physically prepared to undertake

Lead training is a good way to exercise the ferret and get it accustomed to a variety of different environments.

Ferrets are hardy creatures and enjoy exercising in all types of weather.

Placing a carrying box in the ferret run will enable the ferrets to get used to it before they are put in it to go hunting.

I let my ferrets familiarize themselves with purse nets prior to going hunting, and use a vacant warren for this purpose.

a hard day's rabbiting. Another result of training is that a good relationship will have developed between ferret and ferreter. The ferret's temperament and response to handling will have been tested in a variety of settings and the ferreter will have no hesitation when it comes to picking his ferret up. During training the ferret will have been introduced to purse nets. When all of these aims are achieved, the ferret will be ready for work. If only one of them is lacking, both the ferret and ferreter should continue with training.

PLANNING A DAY'S FERRETING

Planning a day's ferreting involves deciding which hunting site to visit, how many and which ferrets to take, and getting all the necessary equipment together.

Deciding Which Hunting Site to Visit

Most ferreters have a number of different hunting sites to choose from. When selecting a specific location for ferreting, four factors influence my choice. Firstly, what stage of the rabbiting season it is. For the first outing of the season I select warrens where I know the growth of vegetation that has taken place through the summer will not stop me getting at the holes. Admittedly, you can use tools such as a scythe to clear the undergrowth, but I prefer to let the onset of the winter weather do this job. Towards the end of the season, I notice the appearance of young rabbits at some warrens sooner than others and will cease to hunt at these warrens before the others.

The second factor is the weather forecast. Although ferreting can be performed in all weathers, and ferreters are amongst the few people who are happy to be out in appalling conditions, there are certain warrens that suit specific weather conditions better than others. By selecting the most appropriate warren, the ferreter will opt for an easier and more comfortable day's hunting. For example, in especially windy weather I choose warrens that I know offer me some shelter and avoid the more exposed sites. Likewise, if it is going to rain heavily, I stay away from warrens that are located in the banks of ditches that fill with water.

Ferrets come in a variety of shades and colours, but this has no effect on their ability to hunt.

64

Thirdly, how numerous are the rabbits? Those places with a high rabbit population may be hunted regularly throughout the season, whereas some warrens only have enough rabbits for occasional visits. You may even come across some small warrens that only warrant a one-off visit.

The final factor to influence my choice of warren is the landowner's preference. On most of the farmland that I have had access to, I have been able to hunt at any time I wanted, but on other ground, such as public schools, I have been limited to weekend visits only. Also, some owners are more eager than others to have their rabbits dealt with.

Deciding How Many and Which Ferrets to Take

This decision is influenced by the size of the warrens that you intend to work. Also consider how difficult the ferret finds a particular warren to hunt in. Other things to bear in mind are the length of time you intend to be hunting and how much work there is for the ferret. If you envisage continuous work from dawn to dusk, you will require enough ferrets to share the load, either by working them together or swapping them over at intervals. If you only intend to be rabbiting for a couple of hours, it is unlikely that you will exhaust the ferrets and therefore replacements will not be required. Do not take so many ferrets along that some of them never get a chance to be worked and are carried about to no avail.

Take into account the experience and particular talents of the ferret. An experienced ferret will succeed in producing a bolt where a novice ferret may not. Consequently, never take a group of inexperienced ferrets by themselves if this can be avoided. As with terriers, the experienced ferret can fulfil the role of 'schoolmaster' and teach the younger, less experienced ferrets. Even amongst my experienced workers I have noticed different strengths that characterize the individual animal's working behaviour. Some of them are more thorough and therefore suit large, deep warrens that require longer to work, whereas those that are quick and heavy enough to seize and maintain hold of a rabbit are selected for more open work, such as under log piles.

Getting all the Necessary Equipment Together

When organizing ferreting equipment for a hunting trip, two mistakes are commonly made. The first is to take along all the equipment the ferreter possesses and generally only ever use half of it. The second is to trim down what is carried to such an extent that there is always something that is needed which has been left at home. If you have long distances to walk, you will resent carrying things that you do not use, but you will find it equally infuriating when you discover that the tool you require is either at home or in the boot of your car, which is parked miles away.

Always think about where you are going to hunt and plan accordingly. For example, I hunt some places where it is not possible to dig and therefore it is pointless taking either a spade or a locator. I also visit locations where there are large extensive warrens requiring every purse net that I possess, while on other ground the medium-sized warrens only require a portion of my nets. When I am ferreting around derelict farm buildings, or where there are a lot of rocks, I take my one-piece metal long spade because it is indestructible and can be used to lever heavy objects out of my way. But when I am on ground where more general digging duties are called for I take my fibreglass drainage spade. This illustrates that the number of nets and particular tools required will vary from one location to another. It also highlights how important it is for the ferreter to be well acquainted with the land that he is going to hunt rabbits on.

It is a good idea to get all the necessary equipment ready on the day prior to the hunt itself. Then you will not be hurried and will have the time and opportunity to ensure that everything is in working order and that there are no tears or holes in the purse nets. Routine chores can also be undertaken, such as dubbing boots and sharpening knives. By preparing in advance you are less likely to leave anything that you might need behind, and there will be no reason for delay in the morning.

I collect my equipment together on the day before a hunt and check that it is all in working order.

CHAPTER 4

THE BASIC FERRETING TECHNIQUE

In order to catch rabbits at a warren the ferreter needs to:

• know how to set nets correctly
• be able to enter ferrets to the warren
• understand and monitor the ferrets' movement below ground
• deal promptly with rabbits caught in purse nets
• know when and how to conduct a dig.

The above knowledge constitutes the basic ferreting technique.

HOW TO SET NETS

In order to catch rabbits successfully, the ferreter must master the skill of netsetting. This rudimentary hunting tool will only perform well if it is set correctly. Netsetting is not a complicated procedure, but requires attention to detail combined with a step-by-step approach. The steps, in sequence, are:

1. Select the appropriate net.
2. Position and secure the net pegs.
3. Lay the net over the hole.
4. Open the net by pulling opposite sides of the net at the same time so that it completely covers the hole.
5. Place the bottom ring in an appropriate position.
6. Check the set nets to ensure that they are holding their positions and have not collapsed.

I look round a warren and make a note of the number of holes before I start setting any nets.

67

Choosing an Appropriate Net

A ferreter will soon realize the benefit of having an assortment of different sized nets at his disposal when he is covering a warren. Rabbits do not build the holes of a warren to a standard size and,

This selection of nets hung in the ferret shed shows that they are available in a variety of sizes and shapes. Certain nets will fit particular holes better than others, and choosing the best net for the job quickly becomes one of the ferreter's talents.

consequently, a 'one size fits all' net will not suit all holes.

If your nets are not big enough to cover a hole, you will either have to abandon working the warren, chance using the ferrets with only half of the holes covered, or set two nets over the hole, which is a fiddly process and not 100 per cent reliable, although it is satisfying when it does work.

Even one medium-sized warren may require the use of nets of various sizes. Selecting the right net is based on observation, which enables the ferreter to estimate the size of the holes and choose an appropriate net. When doing this I always bear in mind that I do not want to use a net that only just stretches to the edges of the bolt hole. I prefer a net that, when it is set, extends a minimum of 2in (5cm) on the ground immediately around the entire bolt hole. It is always easier to set a net that has a larger circumference than the hole as opposed to a net that only just fits. This is because the bigger net is more forgiving when it comes to placing the edges of the net over the contours and bumps of the uneven ground that surrounds the hole.

In addition to the size of the hole, the weather conditions and location should be taken into account when selecting a net. This is because some nets are better suited to certain types of weather than others. For example, I use a heavy hemp net when it is windy because it is better able to keep its position, but I always use nylon nets in the rain because they do not soak up as much water as hemp and will not rot, even if they are not dried properly after use. The location of the warren has an influence on net selection due to the amount of vegetation around the holes. I have ferreted some warrens where it has been difficult to see my green nylon nets amongst the mass of ground cover, and in these cases there is a chance of leaving the odd net behind by mistake. Therefore, it is a good idea to use brightly coloured nets or nets with either a colourful drawcord or painted peg attached to make them stand out amongst the camouflage of dense plants and weeds.

Positioning and Securing the Net Pegs

A net requires secure fixing into the ground by means of a peg in order to function as intended and purse properly around a rabbit. If the peg is loose the force of the bolting rabbit will pull it out of the ground and the net will fail to wrap itself around the rabbit, which will give it time to free itself and escape. If the ferreter is close by, he may be able to seize hold of the drawcord and manually pull the net tight around the rabbit, so preventing its escape. This requires quick responses and great speed and is far from ideal. In short, loose pegs invariably result in lost rabbits.

Standard net pegs measure approximately 16cm in length, and I push about three quarters of the peg's length into the ground to make it secure. In especially loose soil, a longer peg can be employed to obtain a better fixing in the earth. The same advice applies to only leaving a quarter of the peg showing above ground.

The location of the peg when you are setting the net will depend upon the length of the drawcord from the top ring to the peg, and where suitably soft ground for the peg to go in the necessary length can be found. There may be stones, tree roots or other underground obstacles obstructing the path of the peg. In an ideal situation,

the ferreter will place the peg above the bolt hole, but I have known nets to work adequately when the peg has been in a variety of different positions around the bolt hole. However, I strongly recommend looking for a suitable anchor point corresponding to the upper third of the bolt hole. This is because the higher the peg is, the quicker the net will purse around the rabbit. Some bolt holes are on level land with no apparent slope to the hole. In such cases there is no discernible top or bottom to the hole. However, if you look more closely at such a hole, you will usually notice a small mound or bank of earth lining part of the hole. The rabbit uses this feature like a ramp, so that it can make a quick exit from the warren. When faced with a warren that has holes of this type, I advise placing the peg in the ground opposite to the small bank of earth.

In most working situations, it should be possible to drive the pegs into the ground by pushing firmly down with two hands on top of the peg. Nevertheless, there are occasions when the peg can only be driven a quarter or half way in. The heel of the ferreter's boot will provide the extra power to push the peg home. The heel should be placed squarely over the top of the peg and the weight of the body used to exert pressure on the peg as the heel is pressed to the ground. The peg should never be kicked or stamped upon, but simply pressed in one smooth movement. If the ground is exceptionally hard, owing to frost or underlying stones, the ferreter may have to resort to a more drastic method of securing the pegs and use a mallet that has a rubber striker. A couple of strikes with one of these will soon force the peg into the most unyielding ground. The use of rubber on the striker minimizes the amount of noise that the mallet makes so that the rabbits are not deterred from bolting when the nets are set and the ferrets entered.

There are two other methods that I occasionally employ to secure pegs, neither of which requires pushing them into the ground. Although these methods are only used when there is no other alternative, they are worth knowing.

The first could be referred to as the tie method. I discovered this when trying to net a bolt hole that was located at the base of a tree. There was nowhere to push the peg in, but by stretching a length of string around the tree trunk and tying it I had a secure point to which I could easily fasten the net peg. In this way, the tree was acting as the anchor point for the net instead of the peg. I have used this technique many times and it has proved to be very reliable. In a similar manner the peg can be tied to

fence posts and even stock-proof fencing, which nowadays is mechanically stretched and therefore very tense.

The second method is called the wedge method. It basically involves driving the peg between two heavy objects such as rocks. I developed this technique when setting nets over a warren that was partially dug into an old, dry-stone wall. Between the stones there are very narrow gaps into which a peg can be pushed and held firmly enough to enable the net to function effectively. Alternatively, if there are plenty of rocks to hand, the peg can be secured simply by placing a rock of sufficient weight upon it. A rock weighing approximately 10kg should be heavy enough, and I always make sure the rock is up to the task by giving the net a good tug. I regularly use the wedge method for

It is vital to secure net pegs, and I use a mallet to drive pegs into hard ground.

I push at least two-thirds of the peg into the ground to make it secure.

securing net pegs. When set up properly it is very reliable.

Laying the Net Over the Hole

This involves taking hold of the top and bottom rings of a purse net in either hand, stretching it taut and placing it in line with the middle of the bolt hole. The top and bottom rings are then in a position to rest on the ground at the top and bottom of the hole, respectively. They should overlap the hole by a minimum of 4in (10cm) at this stage. If there is no overlap when the net is taut, it will not cover the hole properly when the net is opened.

Opening the Net

Once the net has been laid in the correct position, it can be opened up so that it covers the entire bolt hole and is therefore able to catch any rabbit that tries to escape by this route. Opening the net is a simple process and takes only a few minutes when the hole is a straightforward one. The two edges of the net should be taken in each hand about halfway down their length and then pulled in opposite directions away from the centre of the hole so that they are able to rest on the ground immediately surrounding the hole. This is then repeated at the top and bottom of the net until the entire circumference of the net is resting on the ground bordering the hole. When the net is opened in this way there should not be any slack in the centre of the net causing it to dip inwards down the hole, which may alert a rabbit and prompt it to turn back into the warren instead of bolting. Care should also be taken to ensure that the edges of the net are in close

Once the peg is pushed into the ground, the net is laid over the centre of the hole.

contact to the ground throughout their length and no small gaps are left through which a crafty rabbit may escape. This is a particular problem in ditches where the nets have to be placed in a near vertical position. The problem is compounded by

71

rabbits that are extremely cautious and approach the net very slowly.

Positioning the Bottom Ring

The last stage of setting the net is the correct positioning of the bottom ring. This will vary depending on the layout of the warren where the nets are set. For example, some warrens are flat or gently sloping, while others have steep sides. Therefore, some nets can lie flat in a horizontal position while others have to occupy a more upright or vertical position. The placement of the bottom ring will alter as the net is made to suit the individual contours of the ground at each of the bolt holes.

When setting a net on flat ground, the bottom ring should be placed on the ground that is directly in line with, but opposite to, the top ring, which is fixed to the net peg. If the ring is lying on bare soil, it is customary to push it slightly into the ground. However, where there is plenty of grass or other foliage covering the warren, this is not possible.

The positioning of the ring when the net is covering a hole that is located on a slope depends upon the severity of the slope, which in turn dictates how upright the net needs to be. If the warren is situated on ground that gently slopes, the bottom ring can be positioned as described for flat ground. However, when the incline becomes so severe that the net has a tendency to fall, or when the base of the

The purse net is opened up so that it completely covers the hole.

bolt hole lies flush with the ground, it is customary to put the ring at the bottom of the bolt hole facing inwards where it is pushed into the soft earth. Positioning the ring in this manner helps to maintain the desired shape of the open net so that there are no gaps for the rabbit to escape through.

Checking the Set Nets

After correctly setting one net, systematically go from one hole to another until all the exit holes of the warren are covered. Before entering the ferret, take a walk around the warren and double check that no bolt holes have been missed. It is frustrating to see a rabbit escape through one hole that has been missed when a great deal of time has been spent carefully putting nets over all the other holes. The ferreter should scrutinize his work and ensure that all the nets are still in their set position. There are various reasons why a purse net may be disturbed. These include the weather, especially the wind, the pull of gravity when the warren is on a steep slope, and a novice dog who has not yet realized that it is wrong to thrust his nose into a net that has been set.

Once satisfied that all the holes of a warren are suitably covered, the ferreter is ready to get the ferret out of its carry bag so that it can start work. However, do not expect the ferret to take over operations. On the contrary, the introduction of the ferret is not a replacement of the

In order to make a tidy job of setting the nets, it is often easier to kneel down.

ferreter's labours, but a helpful addition to them. The ferreter still has important decisions to make, and the first of these concerns which hole of the warren to enter the ferret by.

ENTERING THE FERRET

With regard to ferreting, the term 'enter' refers to the deployment of the ferret into the warren. It involves either lifting the corner of a set net and releasing the ferret behind it so that the animal can move into the warren or, alternatively, the net can be left untouched in its set position and the ferret is given help to thread its body through one of the net's mesh spaces into the warren.

Selecting an Entry Point

Does it matter where exactly the ferret is entered into the warren? After all, if there are rabbits to be bolted surely any ferret worth its keep will be able to find them and chase them out. There is an element of truth in this supposition, but it is far from being the whole story. By selecting an entry point based on some rudimentary guidelines, you will make life easier for both your ferret and yourself.

The factors to consider when choosing the best entry point are, firstly, the location of the warren. For instance, is it at the bottom of a hedge, in woodland, on the slope of a hill or in a flat field? Secondly, how much vegetative growth is there at the warren? This will affect the visibility of the bolt holes. Thirdly, are any obstacles present, such as stock-proof fencing, which make it difficult to reach a bolt hole? Even a small warren will have

enough bolt holes to force a choice regarding which one to use to enter the ferret by.

The wisdom of the old ferreters recommended entering the ferret at the lowest point of the warren, and it certainly makes sense to approach the working of a warren in a systematic manner.

During my years of rabbiting with ferrets and purse nets, I have developed my own preferences concerning where to enter the ferret, which I describe below.

When working a warren that runs along a hedge, I always enter the ferret at one end so that it only has one direction in which to move and will progress naturally to the other end of the warren.

When working a warren situated on a slope, I prefer to enter the ferret into the hole at the lowest point of the warren, from where it will move steadily upwards through the various levels of the warren.

When working a warren that is located by a tree, I choose to enter the ferret at the bolt hole that is nearest to the tree trunk so that the ferret will move away from it and, in so doing, drive the rabbits from the area where the largest tree roots are to be found. The importance of this soon becomes evident when the ferreter finds himself in a situation where he has to take up his spade and dig to retrieve his ferret or a rabbit.

If there is a hole that is difficult to get at in any of the locations mentioned previously, I endeavour to enter my ferret to the warren by this hole. By doing this I hope that the ferret will move the rabbits away from this least accessible hole to one that I can reach more easily when the rabbits decide to bolt. Sometimes this may mean dropping the ferret into the midst of a gorse bush or gently chucking it into the centre of a hedge. My ferrets are used to

The entry point (arrow) for the ferret when working a warren that is located in the base of a hedge.

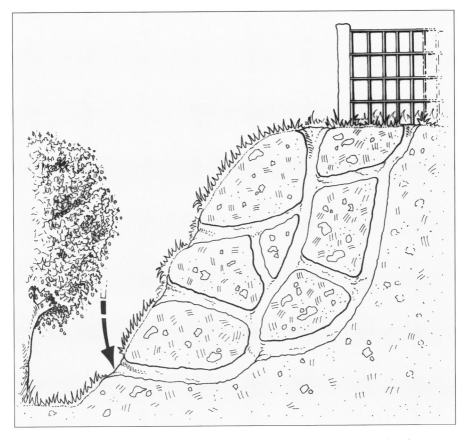

Side view of a warren on a slope with the arrow showing the best entry point for the ferret.

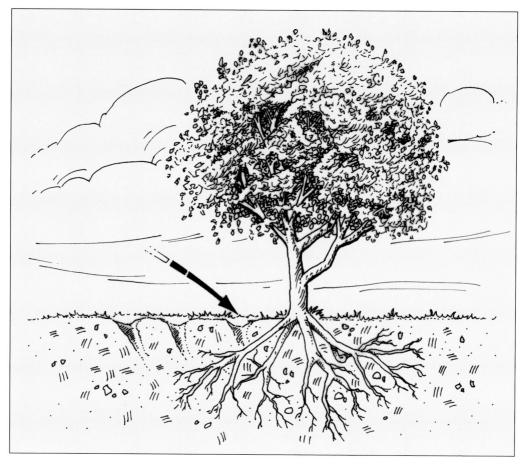

When a warren is located in the shadow of a tree, the best place to enter the ferret is shown by the arrow.

this and they go readily to ground at the desired point.

You may base your decision on where to enter the ferret on the strength of the rabbits' scent, which is detected by a dog with proven marking ability. An experienced rabbiting dog can identify the part of the warren where the rabbits are, particularly when there are not many rabbits in the warren. The dog moves from one hole to another and indicates by its stance, tail movement and even a scraping of the ground with a paw where the rabbits are.

Usually, one or two bolt holes will attract more attention than the others owing to the strength of the rabbits' scent. I am accustomed to watching my Jack Russell terrier do this and will, on most occasions, enter my ferrets through the holes that he has shown most interest in. By doing this, the rabbits usually bolt quicker because the dog has guided the ferret right to where they are.

These are some of the principles that have, in the past, influenced and continue to guide selection of a suitable entry point for the ferret. You will acquire a great deal of knowledge about the warrens where you regularly hunt, and this should be used when making decisions regarding the best way to use your ferret.

How to Handle the Ferret

Never try to enter a ferret to a warren unless it is familiar with being handled and has undergone some form of training to familiarize it with what is going on. When entering less experienced ferrets, the process is as follows (*see* photos on page 78):

1. Hold the ferret around the ribs or belly as opposed to the neck, so that it can be more easily entered on all four paws.
2. Move close to the selected hole and take up a comfortable position, so that you can watch the ferret enter the warren. Usually, the best position for the ferreter is kneeling down by the hole into which the ferret is to be entered.
3. Lift the right-hand corner of the net with the left hand.
4. Place the ferret behind the net in the mouth of the hole, but maintain your hold of the ferret for a few moments.
5. With the ferret facing in the right direction and all its four paws on the ground, relax your hold of the ferret so that it can walk off the hand and into the warren.

If the ferret displays any reluctance, hold it for a bit longer and reposition it slightly further into the mouth of the hole. Should the ferret continue to refuse to enter, either by turning tail or reversing, pick the

Nell, an experienced polecat jill, emerges from the carry bag ready for work.

creature up and give it a calming stroke for a couple of minutes before repeating the process. Sometimes, for no apparent reason, a ferret will not enter no matter how patient or encouraging the handler is. It is essential that force is never used on the ferret.

The philosophical ferreter who rarely loses his cool will try to enter the stubborn ferret down a different hole. However, there is one more trick that can be tried prior to moving to a new location. Entering a steadier ferret first will, in most cases, cajole the reluctant ferret to follow as it abandons its reticence in favour of nosiness. Entering two ferrets down the same hole at the same time is not the desired or best way to work a warren, but it has the advantage of teaching the reluctant ferret

(a)

(b)

(c)

(a–c) The conventional way to enter a ferret to a warren. The ferret should always be handled calmly and gently, even when it puts up resistance to entering the warren. As it becomes more experienced, the ferret may enter under its own steam and will pass through the mesh spaces of the net without disturbing it.

a lesson that will reduce the probability of it behaving likewise on future outings.

Some years ago, one of my ferrets was being particularly awkward when I tried to put him in the warren. In those days I found such displays of stubbornness very frustrating until I decided, partly from desperation and partly from curiosity, to let the ferret do what it wanted and see what happened. It did not propel itself into the warren like a torpedo as I had hoped, but wandered about in the grass for a couple of minutes taking in all the smells.

As I resisted the urge to redirect the wayward ferret, I began to try and see things from the ferret's point of view. Plucked from its cage early in the morning and transferred to a carrying box for as long as it takes to walk or drive to the hunting ground, it is hardly surprising that the creature wants a few moments to itself to stretch its limbs when it is released from its confinement. Once it had satisfied its curiosity, I watched it make a beeline for a net that I had not long since carefully set. I did not have time to dash forward and lift the corner of the net. The ferret went through the mesh space of the net, hardly altering its pace and leaving the net undisturbed.

There is nothing more ridiculous than a ferret twisting about and entangling itself in a purse net. Equally infuriating is having to set nets time and again due to a ferret's clownish behaviour. I learnt that day that if a good-quality net is set correctly, any worthwhile ferret will be able to pass through the net as if it didn't exist. Once it had entered, my ferret got down to work as usual, methodically driving the rabbits from the warren and exiting and re-entering the warren under its own steam.

Since that day I have let my experienced ferrets make their own way into a warren through preset nets. I release them in close proximity to the hole that I would like them to go down and they take care of the rest. Calm, patient endurance, combined with gentle handling and understanding, will inevitably lead to success when entering a ferret, irrespective of which method you employ. I encourage keen ferreters to let their ferrets enter the warren under their own steam by releasing them on the ground nearby. We often comment on the strength of instinct that the ferret possesses to pursue rabbits and, therefore, allowing them more freedom to use these instincts makes sense.

How Many Ferrets Should be Entered to a Warren?

The number of ferrets that are entered to a warren has a direct bearing upon when and how the rabbits bolt. If too many are entered, there is a chance of the rabbits being caught and killed below ground. If too few ferrets are entered, the rabbits can evade the ferret endlessly and, in the unlikely event that a rabbit does bolt, it will have taken the ferret a long time and much hard work.

William Thomas, author of *Rabbit Shooting to Ferrets*, used the size of the warren as his guide to how many ferrets to enter. He recommended the following:

Size of warren	Number of ferrets
Small	1 ferret
Medium	2 ferrets
Large	3 or more ferrets

However, I have noticed that some small warrens that look easy to work are in fact difficult and the ferret has to work hard to force a bolt. Therefore, the degree of difficulty of the warren can be used as an alternative guide to how many ferrets should be entered:

Degree of difficulty	Number of ferrets
Easy	1 ferret
Moderate	2 ferrets
Hard	2 or more ferrets

There are, of course, other factors that influence how many ferrets are entered to a warren. The most important factor is how many ferrets are available for deployment during the day's rabbiting. You also need to consider how many people will be present to watch the ferrets. The more people there are, the easier it will be to keep an eye on the ferrets, which will make multiple entering possible if required. Also bear in mind the capabilities of the individual ferrets that you will be working. For example, one experienced ferret may produce a bolt whereas two novices may struggle. I have two hobs that, if they are entered together in too small a warren, are so quick and strong that they seize and kill the rabbits below ground. Therefore, I only enter one of them in all but the most difficult of warrens.

It is important to avoid entering too many ferrets to a warren. If you enter too few, the ferret has to work extremely hard and the odds are in favour of the rabbit escaping capture. However, when too many ferrets are entered, the tunnels of the warren become congested, making it virtually impossible for the rabbits to find a clear way out. This results in the ferreter having to dig in order to get the rabbits whereas, if the appropriate number of ferrets had been entered, the rabbits would have been able to bolt into the waiting nets. It is a misconception to think that by entering more ferrets you will catch the rabbits quicker.

With experience, the ferreter will learn how a particular warren responds to being worked by a given number of ferrets. This familiarization with the hunting environment is the most reliable method of knowing the right number of ferrets to put into a warren.

A final factor to consider is how many rabbits you want to catch. My hunting philosophy has always been to take only as many rabbits as I need to feed the family, dogs and ferrets. As a result, I am rarely compelled to clear a warren, in one go, of all the rabbits that are in it. The easiest way to achieve this is to enter fewer ferrets than the warren would require if you were undertaking pest control.

Most books on ferreting claim that you need more than one ferret for serious rabbiting. This may give the impression that you need to enter more than one ferret into most warrens in order to catch rabbits. This

has not been my experience. Never underestimate the determination of a ferret when it is hunting, because even by itself it can be effective. I have deliberately placed a lone ferret in a large warren in order to see how well it would get on. In most cases the ferret did bolt a rabbit; however, there were more rabbits in the warren that it could not bolt by itself. The ferret spent a lot of time chasing rabbits below ground, and much effort went into driving successive rabbits out of the warren.

At nearly all the hunting sites that I have visited, I have been able to find warrens that are suitable for one ferret to work. There are tales of poachers and gypsies who needed a quick catch in order to provide food or money, and they often used a single ferret.

Most of the working situations that I have encountered required the entering of no more than three ferrets, and the most common number of ferrets to be entered is two. When using multiple ferrets, only take as many as you can work. I want my ferrets to hunt and work hard and, therefore, always guard against overloading a warren.

If multiple ferrets are to be used at a warren, should they all be entered at the same time or at intervals? Different warrens call for different strategies, and I shall outline my own practice to illustrate one approach.

When working a warren for the first time, I usually enter one ferret to start with and see what happens. If I hear a lot of thumping or rumbling sounds, indicating rabbit movement in the tunnels, or if I see rabbits coming to the nets and turning around instead of bolting, I have no hesitation in entering another ferret. The second ferret is usually entered in the part of the warren where most of the noise and movement is coming from, at the same time ensuring that there is sufficient space between the ferrets so that as they move towards one another there will be room for the rabbits to bolt. If I am working a large warren, or one that runs along a hedgerow, I favour entering two ferrets concurrently at opposite ends of the warren. The ferrets will move systematically towards one another and, in so doing, force the rabbits to bolt in the middle of the warren.

The Ferret's Work in the Warren

When the ferret is entered successfully, its instinctive predatory behaviour is awakened by the strength of the rabbit scent and the environment in which it finds itself.

An experienced ferret displays no signs of fear or nervousness about going into the warren, and as it starts on its way it is quite common to see it lifting its nose in different directions as it inhales the surrounding smells. It is believed that the interpretation of scent is the primary tool that the ferret uses to guide it through the dark tunnels of the warren. I have noticed that the more accomplished workers start off at a much steadier pace than novice ferrets, which are apt to rush through the warren. It is as if they take the time to first get their bearings and then move on their way.

As with all predatory animals, the hunting of quarry is undertaken in a systematic manner, beginning with the location of the prey. It then progresses to the stalking phase, when the hunter moves closer to the intended victim and, finally, to the attack and kill.

The ferret relies on scent to draw it towards the rabbit and follows this aroma-laden pathway as closely as a person would follow footsteps in the sand. However, it will not ignore the detective powers of its other senses. For example, the ferret may receive auditory clues from the rabbit's habit of

This ferret is working its way through the warren and is clearly concentrating on its task.

81

drumming its hind feet on the ground as an alarm signal. This noise can be heard by people stood near the warren. As it continues on its trail, the ferret will catch fleeting glimpses of the outline of a fleeing rabbit. As it draws closer to the rabbit, its senses are increasingly excited and its pace increases. This is why the ferret is sometimes right behind a rabbit that has bolted into the purse net at speed.

A ferret may appear at a bolt hole, sniff the air and turn back into the warren. A crafty rabbit will lead the ferret up and down many avenues of the warren before it finally decides to bolt. Ferrets have the habit of chattering to themselves when they are excited. Consequently, you may hear the chirp of ferret chatter as it pursues the rabbit, and some especially vociferous ferrets start chattering away to themselves as soon as they are entered to the warren and do not stop until the rabbits are caught. In the past, some ferreters, such as the author William Thomas, favoured working ferrets that had a tendency to speak constantly. They believed that this helped to bolt the rabbits more quickly.

There is little the ferreter can do to influence what goes on below ground other than taking up an appropriate watch position, reducing noise to a minimum and keeping still. These simple steps are important, because noise and movement can put a rabbit off bolting and frustrate all the ferret's hard work. The ferreter should position himself so that he can see a given number of bolt holes and still be within a distance that he can easily cover in order to seize hold of the rabbits as soon

Listening at the bolt holes can help inform the ferreter of what is going on within the warren.

as they are caught in the purse nets. When standing in a safe position that is close to the warren you will be able to hear rabbit movement and the drumming of its hind legs upon the ground.

There are some basic guidelines to follow when selecting a suitable watching place. Firstly, it should not fall in a direct line immediately in front of the bolt hole. The bolt hole will face in a given direction, which presents it with a particular outlook. Some rabbits are cautious and move slowly, and before trying to make a dash for safety will pause just inside the purse net and look around to see if they can spot any danger. If a rabbit saw the outline of a human waiting for it, it probably would not bolt. Secondly, do not stand in a position where the wind will blow your scent toward the warren, because this will help to alert the rabbits of your presence.

Ferreters often hunt in company, which means that some form of communication will, at times, be necessary to coordinate the use of the ferrets. I have never enforced a strict no-speaking policy when around a warren, but my brother and I do take the precaution of talking in hushed tones and keeping our conversations to a minimum. When we are at a distance, we use a rudimentary form of sign language to let one another know any vital information.

The ferreter will need to remain still for prolonged periods of time. Do not wander around checking the nets every few minutes in the hope that a rabbit will soon bolt. The shadow that is cast by the roving ferreter over the bolt holes will put rabbits off exiting the warren, as will the sight of a large figure in constant motion. If the ferreter remains still, the rabbits will not be alerted and should have no reluctance to bolt.

When to Investigate Why the Rabbits Have Not Bolted

Most newcomers to the sport ask, 'how long should I wait for the ferrets to bolt the rabbits? Should it be five minutes, ten minutes, quarter of an hour or more?' Unfortunately, there is no standard answer to this question because warrens and conditions can differ dramatically. However, there are some indicators that will help you to make the right decision.

Before we look at these, remember that you should always give your ferret time to do its work. Ferreting requires much patience. There will not always be an innumerable succession of bolting rabbits as soon as the ferret enters the warren. Often the ferrets have to work long and hard to get the rabbits to bolt. The underground tunnels of a warren pose a far greater physical challenge for the ferret than the bolt holes that you have netted suggest, and the ferret will need time to work through these. The best advice is to forget the clock and concentrate on the warren.

We now consider the indicators that help us to know when to draw near and investigate the warren and when to stay away.

If there is any sight of a rabbit moving about within the warren, I tend to stand back and not interfere, because the ferret may still bolt it. The ferreter should keep an eye on the nets so that he can see any rabbits that come to the mouth of the hole but turn back into the warren instead of bolting. This may indicate that the ferret is having trouble getting close enough to the rabbit to force it to bolt and, if the full complement of ferrets is not at work within the warren, the ferreter should consider entering another ferret.

Sometimes I notice the ferret moving through the warren and, if it is doing this with any intent, I remain where I am and let it continue with its work without interference. The ferreter learns to recognize the behaviour of his ferret that demonstrates that it is still hunting in earnest.

If the ferret has exited the warren and no rabbit has bolted, its paws should be inspected for any rabbit fur. A rabbit may sometimes find a tight spot within the warren where it will turn its back on the ferret and remain immovable. The ferret will scratch at the rabbit in an effort to shift it and, in so doing, get rabbit fur stuck in its claws. In such cases the rabbit is still alive and in the warren. Alternatively, the rabbit fur may indicate that the ferret has killed the rabbit underground. To find out if the rabbit is still alive, further investigation is required, which will inevitably result in some digging.

When the rabbits have not bolted and there is no sign of the ferret, it is necessary to take a closer look at the warren. I usually move systematically from one hole of the warren to another, kneeling down at each one so that I can listen for any tell-tale noises and check that none of the nets have been pushed aside. The absence of any sounds or movement is a clue that the ferret is having difficulty making the rabbit bolt. Before starting to dig, most ferreters will make a sweep of the warren with a locator to ascertain if the ferret is stationary and, if so, where it has stopped. There are other ways of determining where exactly the ferret is in the warren, but these are used infrequently nowadays owing to the popularity of locators. My brother and I are included in the minority of ferreters who never use a locator. We have developed a method that relies solely on the acute senses of our dogs. It is described in detail in the section on digging (*see* page 89).

WHAT TO DO WHEN THE RABBIT IS CAUGHT IN THE NET

When a ferret is in a warren, the resident rabbits' primary instinct is to flee, and in the process of trying to escape they rush into the waiting purse nets with such momentum that the nets pull tight and wrap themselves around the rabbits. The ferreter should act quickly and decisively in dealing with the rabbits in the nets. This is only possible if all the nets have been set in view. Sometimes a single person cannot oversee all the nets due to the size or shape of a warren, and in such cases it is useful to have another person present to offer assistance. It is important that any caught rabbits are picked up as soon as possible because, once in the net, a rabbit is momentarily stunned and remains still for a short period of time. The rabbit should not be left to struggle with the net and panic.

The ferreter's focus should be on dealing with the rabbit. When I first took up ferreting, my mind was as much on retrieving my ferret as it was on dealing with the rabbit. I soon realized that my ferret was not intent on running off or trying to escape, and I was able to relax and take care of one task at a time. The purse net is a very effective tool and will easily hold the rabbit for the few moments that it takes the ferreter to move from his watch post to the bolt hole. Therefore, there is no need for the ferreter to run. A brisk walking pace will suffice and has the benefit of creating less commotion and noise.

As mentioned earlier in the book, I always secure hold of the rabbit by the loins and dispatch it while it is still in the net. This task takes minutes to complete, and as soon as the rabbit is killed it is placed out of the way so that I am able to redirect

A purse net in operation. The net slides along the tightened drawcord and wraps around the rabbit.

my attention to the warren. If the ferret has remained in or re-entered the warren, I quickly set a net over the bolt hole to replace the one that has pursed around the rabbit. I carry one or two nets in my pocket for this purpose. They are always at hand when needed, and it is quicker to lay one of these than to remove the dead rabbit from the net and re-use it.

If the ferret has exited the warren, I pick it up after I have finished dealing with the rabbit. However, when I am ferreting with my brother we divide our labour so that one of us can dispatch the rabbit while the other concentrates on retrieving the ferret. Sometimes the ferret is only momentarily behind the bolting rabbit, which it is trying desperately to catch. Consequently, its mind is focused on the rabbit and it may become confused when its prey is lifted off the ground in front of it. In such cases the ferret will usually move around in a few small circles with its nose pointing upward in an effort to detect the scent and

When the task is completed, the hind legs should look as shown here.

To leg a rabbit, first make a cut approximately 4cm long in the space between the bone and tendon of the hind leg above the hock or elbow. The foot of the opposite hind leg is inserted into this hole and then pulled through until the hocks lock against one another.

location of the rabbit. Even if the ferret moves away from the ferreter, it will not travel far in the time that it takes to deal with a rabbit. Those ferrets that are familiar with a 'call' sound can be redirected or stopped in their tracks when the signal is given. When the work in the warren is completed, I sometimes let my ferret wander about freely. I only give the ferret this freedom if the surrounding environment is clear of hazards and dense cover, and therefore I can keep an eye on it. While the ferret entertains itself, I collect the nets and attend to other tasks such as the peeing and legging of the rabbits that have been caught.

Peeing or thumbing refers to the process of expelling urine from the bladder, and it is best done when the rabbit is still warm.

A rope is being used to tie rabbits together so that they can be carried easily over a shoulder.

The bladder is emptied to prevent the possible contamination of the meat with urine should the bladder be accidentally damaged during the course of gutting and skinning the rabbit. It involves placing the thumb of one hand on the centre of the lower part of the rabbit's abdomen, with the fingers of the same hand gripping the corresponding part of the spine. This hand is then moved downwards towards the tail with firm pressure applied throughout the movement. The urine will either stream or trickle out, depending on how full the bladder is. The ferreter should remember to point the rabbit away from his body when performing this task.

Legging is the process whereby one hind leg of the rabbit is threaded through the other by means of a vertical 2cm cut that is made just above the hock. This provides the ferreter with a convenient and effective way to carry the rabbits as he moves from one warren to another, and when he is working his ferrets the rabbits can easily be hung over a branch of a nearby tree or a fence post. The correct position of the cut is easy to see and feel. Starting at the foot of a hind leg, move your hand upwards until you reach the first major joint, which has a feeling reminiscent of an elbow and is, in fact, the hock. At the back of the leg, immediately above the hock, is a length of fibrous material that has an elastic feel. This is a tendon and connects the muscles of the upper leg with the bones of the lower leg. Parallel with the tendon is a long bone, and in between the two is a narrow depression, which is where the cut should be made. A narrow pointed blade is ideal for this. Care should be taken to avoid making the hole any bigger than that needed to push the opposite paw through. The ferreter soon becomes expert at performing the above tasks and will be able to accomplish them in the field in a matter of minutes.

UNDERTAKING A DIG

When to Dig

Ferreting revolves around the warren and, therefore, it is not surprising that sooner or later the ferreter will be faced with a situation when he has to dig into the warren. In the following situations the ferreter will need to dig:

- when the rabbit will not bolt
- when the rabbit has been killed within the warren
- when the ferret is trapped below ground.

There are opposing views concerning digging. Some people consider it one of the most interesting parts of the sport, but for others it is nothing more than a necessary chore. Digging has been an integral part of ferreting for many years. In old photographs of ferreters, there is invariably a spade somewhere in the picture.

I was a late convert to digging. For years I shunned this aspect of ferreting and had a 'no dig' policy. In my defence, this did suit the sites I hunted on at the time because the ferrets were 100 per cent effective at producing a clean bolt. Therefore, I had no need to resort to a spade.

Since relocating to the northeast of Scotland, I have reassessed my views about the usefulness of digging. The rabbits in Scotland are not nearly as willing to bolt as their southern brethren. If I did not use a spade on the land where I now hunt, at least one fifth of a season's catch would be left behind. I am now convinced that digging plays a significant part in enhancing the rabbit-catching abilities of the ferreter. I had always thought that digging was a slow and particularly boring aspect of ferreting, but a successful dig can be satisfying and, in some respects, even quite exciting.

Where to Dig

How will the ferreter know where to start digging? To avoid moving a lot of soil, you need to pin-point the location of the ferret with a very small margin of error. This will enable the ferreter to concentrate his efforts on one place. It will also enable the ferret to be found more quickly and diminish the degree of disruption to the warren.

The most common and modern way to determine the ferret's position within the warren is to use a piece of equipment often referred to as a 'locator', although it may be advertised for sale as a 'ferret finder'. This comprises a ferret collar in which there is a transmitter, and the ferret's progress can be monitored by means of a receiver operated by the ferreter. He should be able to detect with a fair degree of accuracy when the ferret is moving and when it is stationary. By highlighting the position where the ferret is still, the locator helps the ferreter to determine the correct place to start digging.

The blade of the spade cutting into the warren can sometimes generate enough disturbance to prompt a stubborn rabbit to move. Therefore, the locator should be left on the ground where the ferreter is digging so that any movement of the ferret can be identified immediately. The ferreter will then be able to decide whether to continue digging or stop and wait until either the ferret settles or the rabbit bolts. The main advantage of the electronic locator is its precision, which means that only a single hole needs to be dug to get to the ferret and trapped rabbit.

However, locators are not the only option. Traditional methods were employed long before locators were ever dreamt of. I remember reading Fred J. Taylor's contribution on ferreting to Jack Charlton's book, *Field Sports*, in which he points out that, although he was in possession of two electronic locators, he seldom used them. Howard G. Glynn, in his excellent book, *Net-making for Sport*, states that at the time he wrote the book he routinely used a locator, but he admits that he coped perfectly well for years without one. For those who are wondering how anyone could possibly manage without a locator, the answer is the line ferret. Prior to locators, using a line ferret was the most popular way to ascertain where a rabbit was cornered or where ferrets were laid up on a dead rabbit. As the title implies, the ferret, which was always a hob, was attached to a long thin leash that had markers along its length to indicate how much of the material was being unravelled when in use.

The ferret was entered to the warren and the line fed out in response to its movement. When the ferret came to a standstill, recognized by the absence of any pulling on the lead, the ferreter could determine approximately how far away it was and the general direction in which the ferret had travelled. A series of strategically spaced holes were then dug using the lead as a guide.

In the British Field Sports Society's *Guide to Ferreting* by Samuel and Lloyd, the writers state that the task of the line ferret is to dissuade other ferrets from lying up and to lead the ferreter in digging through the dark maze of burrows to the point of a kill. In order to accomplish this, the line ferret had to be willing to remain with the kill until it was reached by digging. Because it was attached to a lead, the line ferret was under the control of the ferreter, and in areas where the rabbits were known to bolt badly the ferret was nearly always worked on a line. Some were reputedly trained to hold on to the rabbit and draw it out of the warren. There are tales of lost ferrets being pulled out of holes by the scruff of the neck by line ferrets.

The ferreter may guide his digging with a rabbiting dog, which will mark the locations where rabbits can be found. The dog's phenomenal scenting abilities enable it to differentiate between a warren that is populated with rabbits and one that is not. My terrier can detect rabbits in some unusual and challenging environments, such as derelict farm buildings and barns full of ancient crumbling bales of straw. To test the dog's talents, my brother and I once set him the task of locating the whereabouts of the ferrets and rabbits within a warren when no bolts were forthcoming. He took on this new responsibility with the manic enthusiasm typical of working terriers. He certainly deserved full marks for his energetic efforts and, judging from his tenacious manner and expression, nothing short of success would satisfy him.

The terrier began by sniffing every hole of the warren in order to ascertain which one offered the strongest scent. No other dog can move around a warren with the

89

A rabbiting dog is capable of using its scenting powers to assist the ferreter in his search for rabbits.

speed and balance of a terrier, and he quickly identified the most promising hole, which he showed to us using a variety of behavioural traits. These included tense posture, vigorous tail movement, scraping the earth with his paws, inserting his nose into the hole and the inevitable grumbling. We followed his leading and began a multiple dig but, instead of being guided by a long line, we relied on the dog's detection and accurate interpretation of the rabbit scent.

The terrier was invited into each hole that was dug in order to use his nose. He showed us, by the scraping of his paws and direction of his body, which way we should continue digging. As we dug our way closer to the rabbit, the terrier's mannerisms became more intense and in his excitement he succumbed to giving voice. When this happens, instead of digging another hole, we broaden the one we are on until we can reach the rabbit. If, at any time during the dig, we deviated from the most direct route to the rabbit, the terrier made our error obvious by his total lack of interest.

Although using the terrier in this way was intended as an experiment, all the parties involved enjoyed it so much that we decided to adopt it as our principal means of detecting where to dig. With the benefit of more practice we have honed our skills and become more efficient. My brother was quick to notice the value and potential of having a canine locator and, as a result, devised a training programme for his two haughty collies. He learnt that training a dog to locate ferrets and rabbits below ground takes time, a lot of patience and a great deal of empathy with the dog.

The first step is to get the dog interested in rabbits by taking it to an area where there are always plenty of rabbits above ground that can be easily seen and safely chased. The instant the dog shows any interest it is allowed to give chase. Some dogs will pursue the rabbits the first time they see them, while others are more reticent and may need the help of an older dog to show them the ropes. Encouraging a keenness for rabbits is the foundation for teaching a dog to locate them, and the handler should provide the dog with plenty of time and instruction. Once it is firmly established in the dog's mind that rabbits are their intended quarry, the training can move to a warren.

When pursuing rabbits the dog will eventually chase one to ground, and it may try to enter the burrow to continue the chase or it may scratch away at the burrow in an attempt to dig out the rabbit. Whichever of these techniques the dog adopts, it should be praised so that it learns that the game is not over once the rabbit has gone to ground. When the dog stops trying to enter the burrow or ceases digging, it should be taken to every hole of the warren where it can be encouraged to continue the search by the handler asking, 'What have you got?' in an excited tone of voice. The slightest change in the dog's behaviour should be noted when doing this.

Summer is the best time to begin the dog's training because there are plenty of rabbits above ground lazing in the sun. Summer is also the time when the traditional ferreter's hunting activities have come to an end and so he has plenty of time to train his dog. The dog will benefit from being taken out at least once a week to a location where it is allowed to chase the rabbits to ground and examine the holes of the warren in search of scent. It may take some time to develop the skill of interpreting the dog's intricate body language that it displays when working and when it has found a rabbit. The position of the ears, movement of the tail, vocal sounds and a quivering body are some of the signals to watch out for. The handler may also feel the dog's tension by placing his hands on its body. When a dog has a strong scent, the muscles of its body will be very tense.

In order to create such an understanding between you and your dog, it is best to get the rabbiting dog as a puppy. You can then observe it as it grows and matures. The ferreter will need to be aware of how his dog responds to different stimuli. For example, how does the dog react when it first detects the scent of a rabbit and what differences in behaviour does it exhibit when it has finally tracked down a rabbit? With practice, the ferreter will be able to read the many vital clues that his dog gives just as quickly and easily as a person hears the pips of an electronic locating device.

Working dog owners must permit their dog to take control of the dig because it can read any scent emitting from a warren. My brother and I are happy to act simply as spade operators and let the dogs lead a dig. When we have the humility and common sense to work with dogs in this fashion, remarkable results can be achieved.

How to Conduct a Dig

The intention of a dig is to retrieve a ferret and rabbit in a way that does not cause unnecessary disruption to the warren. The reason for this is twofold. Firstly, to leave the warren in a state that rabbits can continue to live in and, secondly, out of consideration for the landowner who has given permission for the ferreter to hunt on his ground. If the likelihood of needing to dig was not fully explained when first obtaining rabbiting rights, it may be wise to ask the owner first before cutting the ground with a spade. Rabbit warrens are a natural part of the countryside, and the ferreter should aim to leave the countryside as he found it so that there are no perceptible signs of him having been there.

Before beginning a dig, bear in mind that once you have got the rabbit your work is not at an end. The holes will require back filling and the ground will need levelling. Do not start digging unless you are prepared to do this. For best results I suggest

that you employ a spade with a narrow, long blade. First make a cut in the earth approximately 1ft (30cm) square and 3–4in (8–10cm) deep. This can then be levered up with the spade and placed to one side so that it can be replaced in the same position when the dig is complete. A circular hole can now be dug down to the required depth. For those warrens where the tunnels run no more than 3ft (90cm) below the surface, the hole only needs to be wide enough for a rabbit to be pulled through. In these cases you can use your arm to reach down and secure hold of the rabbit. When the tunnels lie deeper below the ground than this, the rabbit will be beyond arm's length and the hole will have to be widened to enable the ferreter to get more of his body into it. The spade

Every ferreter should know when it is appropriate to dig into a warren and should conduct the dig in a systematic and careful manner.

should be used with care when the ferreter reaches the stage where he is about to break into the tunnel of the warren. The reason for caution is to prevent the last few inches of soil that needs removing or the walls of the tunnel from collapsing on the ferret. Sometimes my brother and I resort to using our hands to remove the last bit of loosened soil, particularly if we are working on shallow warrens. Following retrieval of the ferret and rabbit, backfill all the holes that have been dug, replace the first cut and level the surface so that the ground is left in a tidy condition.

Problems when Digging

Nearly every ferreter can tell you about a dig that has gone wrong. Many problems may be encountered when digging into a warren. Even after accurately locating the ferret and rabbit, the ferreter does not know what lies between him and them until he cuts into the ground. There may be rocks or tree roots blocking his way. The soil may be heavy and claggy, or loose and liable to collapse. When meeting obstacles the ferreter can either dig around them or physically remove them. I can usually lever rocks out of the way with my long-handled metal spade. When I encounter peripheral tree roots, rather than striking at them with a spade, I clear the soil around them and use a folding saw to cleanly cut the portion of root that is in my way; this does not harm the tree. If digging in loose, unstable soil, it is advisable to sink a long metal probe through the soil before digging commences so that you are aware of the depth of the tunnel and can rediscover it quickly if the soil does collapse.

The position of the warren may prove a hindrance to digging. Not all warrens are located on flat land with plenty of room for the ferreter to move round the hole he is digging. If the branches of bushes, hedges or trees are in the way they should only be removed if permission has been given. This task should be done sympathetically with a proper tool such as a saw. Never resort to pulling or twisting branches off. Some of the warrens that I have dug into are located on steep slopes. The safest way to dig in this situation is with a short-handled spade. This tool allows me to rest one knee constantly on the ground, thus lowering my centre of gravity and keeping my body well forward while I am digging so that I am less likely to lose my balance and fall.

Needless to say, the weather can play havoc with a dig. Heavy rain can rapidly turn soil into slippery mud, making digging difficult and uncomfortable.

The process of the dig itself may disturb the rabbit so that it moves away from the position where the dig commenced. It may either go deeper into the warren or chance a bolt. Being aware that this might happen, the ferreter should take the precaution of leaving all the purse nets set in place during the course of the dig so that the rabbit is caught if it does decide to bolt.

There are times when a dig will have to be abandoned, either because the rabbit moves too deeply into the warren or the ferreter meets some immovable obstruction. When this happens the first priority is to get the ferret back safely. This is why, throughout its upbringing, the ferret should have been trained to respond to some form of call or signal. Apart from calling the ferret and placing a couple of dead rabbits at the holes to tempt it out, the only other option is to use a line ferret, which is bigger and more forceful than the loose workers and therefore capable of driving them off the rabbit.

When line ferrets were commonly used in this way some years ago, many of them were taught to recognize that a couple of tugs on the line was the signal for them to exit the warren.

Some ferrets respond more readily than others, and this is one of those occasions when the ferreter has to exercise a great deal of patience. When there are a number of people ferreting together it is possible to divide forces so that one person takes responsibility for keeping watch for the ferret while another takes the opportunity to set the purse nets at the next warren that is to be worked.

However, the foremost priority is to retrieve the ferret. Regardless of how long it takes or how frustrating it is, someone should always be at the warren awaiting the ferret's appearance.

Skills Required by the Ferreter

- The ability to handle ferrets
- A general understanding of wildlife and, in particular, the ways of rabbits
- The ability to set nets in various environments
- The ability to discern and comprehend the signs and sounds that occur when the ferret is working
- The ability to humanely kill rabbits
- The knowledge of how to dig when necessary
- The ability to work dogs in conjunction with ferrets
- Patience and a willingness to allow the ferret adequate time to do its work
- Perseverance in order to work those warrens that require a lot of time, effort and thought

CHAPTER 5

THE ADVANCED FERRETING TECHNIQUE

DEFINITION

The advanced ferreting technique is used when working ferrets at those locations that differ from the typical warrens that the ferreter is accustomed to. For instance, it shows you how to proceed when all the holes of a warren cannot be netted, and how to work the ferret under a shed, amongst a log pile and loose above ground in conjunction with dogs. The advanced ferreting technique is essentially concerned with the employment of ferrets in unusual places. It relies on a more creative approach to the setting of nets, combined with a willingness to allow the ferret to engage its hunting instincts in a more varied way, than that described in Chapter 4. Greater demands are placed on the ferret, both physically and mentally, but the ferret seems to relish new challenges, and rewards trust in its ability with a determination to hunt that enables the ferreter to catch rabbits in places he would usually ignore.

The technique described in this chapter is well within the capability of any persistent ferreter in possession of a sound working ferret. Although many ferreters are not often faced with the problematic sites that require the advanced ferreting technique, on those occasions when they do have the opportunity to use it they will find that, as well as adding a new dimension to their sport, it is immensely satisfying to succeed at catching rabbits in a location where the odds are very much stacked in favour of them escaping.

HOW TO USE FERRETS IN A WARREN LOCATED IN A STONE WALL

Long before stock-proof fencing was in existence, farmers relied on locally available materials to enclose their fields, mark their boundaries and keep their livestock in. For many, and particularly those occupying northern areas of Britain, this meant fashioning innumerable rocks and boulders into stone walls. Many of these walls were built hundreds of years ago and, sadly, some of them have fallen into a state of decline.

In the northeast of Scotland, where I live, the once proud walls that surround old crofts and their steadings now boast a number of small rabbit warrens along their length. The rabbits have been able to shape tunnels in the wall out of the cavities that exist between the broad rocky building blocks. These walls possess a surprising amount of usable room for the rabbit, which is dry and affords protection from predators.

These rocks and boulders are ideal hiding places for rabbits, but they can be worked with some creative net setting and a versatile ferret.

At first sight these walls present a working challenge no different from a typical hedge bottom and, as both structures were intended for the same function, they bear a marked resemblance with regard to the amount of ground that they occupy and their typical location on the margins of fields and around farm buildings. The problems involved in using ferrets in a stone wall soon become apparent when the purse nets are brought out. To start with, there is no soft ground to push the pegs into, and it is necessary to use the wedge method mentioned in Chapter 4. It takes longer than the conventional method and some pegs may require several strikes with the mallet to ensure that they are held fast. Another complication is obscured bolt holes, caused by the stacking of unwanted fence posts, wire and other rubbish against the wall. In these cases, purse nets should be carefully placed over and around the abandoned objects in order to prevent escape through what might look like an inconsequential gap between posts lying next to one another. Rabbits are able to squeeze themselves through incredibly small gaps. As an alternative to placing nets over fence posts and the like, a trained rabbiting dog can be used to guard these areas and seize any rabbit that tries to escape via this route. Terriers are ideal for this type of work.

I always enter my ferret through any obstacles first, so that the rabbits are driven away from bolting in this direction. Digging is impracticable when working a warren located in a stone wall, and for this reason, and because the warrens themselves tend to be quite small, I usually enter only one experienced ferret. This practice virtually eliminates the incidence of rabbits being killed within the warren or being backed into a corner and refusing to bolt.

As with a hedge, a stone wall ideally suits two lookouts, one stationed either side of the wall. If available, dogs can be usefully employed on both sides of the wall where their task is to pick up, or drive back into the nets, any rabbits that try to escape. They should be given the freedom to work under their own initiative if they are to be effective.

WORKING FERRETS AMONGST ROCKY OUTCROPS

What is a Rocky Outcrop?

A rocky outcrop is a collection of rocks heaped into a mound. They can occur naturally but are mostly man-made. For example, farmers often tip unwanted building materials and rocks that have been cleared from their fields in an area that is not suitable for grazing or sowing. Some rocky outcrops are the product of fallen farm buildings and, as a result, they vary enormously in size. Some may occupy a hillside, while others are no bigger than a garden feature. Some consist of rocks that can be manually moved out of the way if necessary, while others contain huge rocks that can only be lifted with a crane.

These rather haphazard structures provide the rabbit with an impressive defence against predators. As a result, they are often used as temporary hideaways when a threat is present, which includes the ferreter. From my own experience I have noted that rocky outcrops are more common in the north of England and Scotland.

Working the Site

The principal difficulties that a rocky outcrop presents to a ferreter are, firstly, that digging is impossible and moving the rocks when they are light enough can put the ferret in a precarious position unless great care is taken. Therefore, it is virtually impossible to retrieve the ferret from the majority of rocky outcrops, and it has to

---

The Ferreter's Code of Conduct

- Always put the welfare of the ferret first
- Do not forget to close gates behind you
- Do not disturb livestock
- Do not trespass
- Do not poach
- Tidy up after digging holes
- If you paunch rabbits in the field, bury the entrails
- Treat the countryside that you have access to with respect and show consideration for wildlife
- Keep dogs under control at all times
- Be polite at all times and leave the farmer a few rabbits for his dinner

be relied upon to exit and return to the ferreter of its own accord. Secondly, the indiscriminate piling of these rocks results in a myriad of gaps through which the rabbit can bolt to freedom. Many of these gaps appear too narrow for a rabbit to squeeze through, but experience has taught me that the rabbit is capable of getting through unbelievably tight gaps. The ferreter is well advised to not overlook these. Therefore, many nets are required when working a rocky outcrop, and placing all the nets can be a time-consuming task. Thirdly, it is difficult to secure the net pegs firmly. They either have to be wedged in place between the rocks or a suitably weighted rock must be put on each of the pegs. Finally, working in this type of environment is extremely demanding on the ferret, which will have to do a lot of running, climbing, twisting and turning.

Assessing a Rocky Outcrop's Suitability for Work with Ferrets

I use my ferrets regularly at a location that is referred to by the locals as the 'quarry'. As you would imagine, it is composed principally of boulders and rocks. Some of these are heaped into little mounds, but there is also a more extensive area where large rocks cover a sizeable slope. Nearly every time I visit this site I watch the rabbits scamper away into these rocky catacombs. Some of them have been dug out so that they form warrens with grand fortified rock entrances, but often the rabbits simply use the natural cavities between and under the rocks as a hideaway. When deciding whether or not to use my ferrets to bolt the rabbits from the rocks in the quarry, I consider the following factors.

1. How safe it is for the ferret. This is my first priority. There is little sense in pursuing a rabbit at the expense of losing a ferret. An accurate understanding of your ferret's hunting capabilities and its physical prowess will help you decide. Ferrets are amazing athletes and very determined hunters. Rather than shying away from strenuous work, my ferrets thrive on doing their job in the most challenging of environments.

2. How extensive the formation of rocks is. When the rocks cover a large area of ground or are deeper than a man's height they are classified as unsafe and disqualified from being worked. The odds are tipped too much in the rabbits' favour and there is an increased likelihood of the ferrets encountering real difficulty and the ferreter being unable to do anything to help them.

3. Whether I can see a clear way in and out for the ferrets, and also see the ground upon which the rocks are resting. I also like to have some vision of the main pathways or chambers within the rocks that the rabbits use.

Using the Ferrets

Ferrets can be used effectively at a rocky outcrop to bolt the rabbits into purse nets, into the path of waiting dogs or so that they flee to a nearby warren that can be more easily worked. The preparations that are made prior to entering the ferret will depend upon which of these options is selected.

When setting nets, the gaps between the rocks should be treated as if they were bolt holes. With the net stretched over the gap it should overlap the rocks surrounding the hole by at least 10cm. When laid against rocks, the nets usually hold their shape quite well in all types of weather. This is because the fibres of the net cling to the rough edges of the rocks. As mentioned earlier, it can be difficult to secure the pegs. However, thanks to the haphazard construction of these mounds, there are plenty of usable anchor points for the pegs where rocks knit untidily together. I would guess that when setting nets at these locations about 80 per cent of the pegs are secured by wedging them in place. The remainder are held firm by hefty rocks, which are retrieved from the ground and lifted on to each of the pegs.

Whether I want to bolt the rabbits into purse nets or for waiting dogs, I always enter my ferret in the part of the mound where my terrier has displayed his most persistent mark. This is where the scent is at its strongest and, therefore, the ferret is placed in close proximity to the rabbit.

When deploying the ferret with the intention of bolting rabbits to a nearby warren, I first set nets over the holes of the warren so that the rabbits can be caught in them as they attempt to dash underground. In those cases when I choose not to employ purse nets, I let my terrier enter those outer chambers of the rocky outcrop where he is able to squeeze his body. The terrier is ideally suited to moving at speed in this kind of environment. Its innate opportunistic hunting skills produce results as the ferret drives the rabbits away from the centre of the maze of rocks into the path of the dog.

Two items of equipment, which are especially helpful to the ferreter when working this location, are a torch to enable him to see further into the rocky structure than his unaided eye will allow and a long-handled one-piece metal spade, which is ideal for levering heavy rocks out of the way when necessary. Rocky outcrops are settings that suit the quickest and most athletic of ferrets. They must combine their resolute

Wedging a net peg between two rocks will hold it secure when working at locations such as the one shown in the photograph on page 96.

99

determination to catch rabbits with a willingness to come to hand once the rabbits have bolted.

USING FERRETS UNDER SHEDS

Sheds are a common sight in gardens throughout the country, and offer various opportunities to the rabbits. Some easy digging out will allow them to get comfortably under the floor. This is particularly easy with sheds that are raised up on bricks or the like, since all they have to do is dig a couple of semi-circular half holes, which they can then use as entry and exit points. A shed offers rabbits a safe, dry place to hide, which is invariably close to vegetable patches.

When ferreters are called in to tackle the damage caused to plants and vegetables by rabbits, the rabbits are often traced back to an out-of-the-way shed that is rarely used or visited. At one of the locations where I hunt there is a cottage that is rented out and therefore empty for lengthy periods of time. An assortment of old sheds that have not been used for years are scattered around the cottage. My attention was drawn to these when I noticed that the rabbits that I was hunting in a nearby field were bolting towards the cottage and disappearing from sight. I followed their path to a large old shed with some giveaway diggings at its base. I did not have to look any further to discover where the rabbits had gone.

There are certain things that are worth noting about these locations and the rabbits that occupy them. Firstly, you are not likely to find a lot of rabbits under a shed at the same time. The most I have seen is five, but one or two is more common. Secondly, there is only a minimal amount of net setting required as the rabbits rarely establish a lot of entrance holes under the shed and it is quite unusual for them to link their diggings up with a proper warren or a system of distant hidden bolt holes. The extent of their digging is invariably the four sides of the shed. Thirdly, as with a lot of the hunting locations described in this chapter, the ferreter will not be able to start a dig of any description. Some sheds may be small enough to be lifted out of the way if necessary, but most people are not keen on this option, and if the sheds are full, which they usually are, there will be no chance of moving it. If the ferret is unable to produce a clean bolt, a different approach is needed. This depends on the size of the shed.

The most common sizes of sheds are 6ft × 4ft (180cm × 120cm) and 8ft × 6ft (180cm × 240cm), which means that the average ferreter is able to reach a long way underneath to retrieve a rabbit that will not bolt or has been killed by the ferret. If two ferreters are present, they should be able to reach every corner under small and medium-sized sheds. Some earth can be scraped out at the base of the shed to enable more freedom of movement for the outstretched arm. A torch is useful because it helps the ferreter to see what is going on beneath the shed floor and prevents him feeling around in the dark with his hands. It is essential that the ferreter has confidence in the ferret he works, and trusts that it will not take offence to a hand retrieving either it or a rabbit from in front of it when it is underneath a shed. It is certainly not the environment in which to work a ferret that is likely to get over-excited.

Steps can be taken to increase the chance of a clean bolt. Firstly, be as quiet as possible in your movements, preparations and entering of the ferret. This is especially important when hunting under sheds because the ferreter is never standing very far from the rabbit. Secondly, when a rabbit has bolted to the shed from a nearby field, give it time to settle itself before entering the ferret. A rabbit will be reluctant to bolt if it is still pumped full of adrenalin and feels the presence of a threat close at hand. Give the rabbit time to think that the threat has passed and it is safe. Thirdly, only enter one steady ferret. There are no deep caverns under the shed and it is counterproductive to overload such a small working area with ferrets. The deployment of too many ferrets will result in the rabbit being killed beneath the shed before it has time to bolt.

Some ferreters may question whether this kind of activity is worth the effort, owing to the small numbers of rabbits present at this location. However, the net setting is easy and it does not take long to work the ferret under a shed. It also provides variation to ferreting at a warren and is much appreciated by gardeners.

FERRETING IN A WOODPILE

A woodpile is defined as logs, planks, pallets or any scrap wood that has been stacked with the intention of being cut for firewood. On a farm, a woodpile may refer to unwanted wood of all descriptions that has been dumped together in a remote place. There are different types of wood-piles on some of the ground where I regularly hunt. I would have ignored them had I not noticed that the rabbits were scuttling off to these various woodpiles rather than to their established warrens. After much observation I noticed that some of the rabbits were choosing to live amongst the woodpiles.

I needed to find an efficient way to hunt at such a location. However, to be successful, there were a number of hurdles to overcome. The first of these was the absence of clearly identifiable rounded bolt holes that are common to warrens and make it obvious where to put the nets. The rabbits had not made any diggings and relied on the spaces that naturally occur when wood is piled on the ground and on top of itself to find their way into the pile. Hence, there were an enormous variety of escape routes in a reasonably small area and netting them all was a fiddly process; most of the nets could only be secured by wrapping the pegs around, or tying the drawcords to, a piece of wood. I could have rolled out a long net at a suitable distance to catch the bolting rabbits, but I wanted to see what results I could achieve with purse nets.

There are two approaches to working ferrets in a woodpile that I have used with some success. With the first method, all the openings visible on the exterior of the pile are covered with a purse net. I use my smaller nets for this purpose because the holes are rarely very big. This approach suits one or two ferrets best when they are used solely in conjunction with purse nets. When a single ferret is used, I enter him at one end of the pile so that he can work systematically along the length of it. When two ferrets are worked they can be entered at opposite ends of the wood-pile at the same time so that they can clear the woodpile of rabbits as they move towards one another. In the latter case, the most likely place for a bolt to occur is at the mid-section of the pile, and the ferreter should concentrate his attention here.

The second method is less organized, but can work well if the ferreter has the

When ferreting in woodland, a net peg can be secured by tying it to a length of nylon that is tied to a tree trunk.

the rabbits that appear in the section of the pile where there are no nets. The terrier will either seize hold of a rabbit that is attempting to flee or turn it back into a net or the ferret.

An experienced rabbiting dog has highly tuned senses, which help it to accurately detect where the rabbits are and where they are most likely to emerge. The dog knows, without the need of commands, where best to position himself and when is the ideal time for him to make his move. Terriers are the perfect size for this type of work and are often able to force themselves into the outer layer of the woodpile. They make the most of every opportunity that they get and possess the quick reactions that the task requires. The benefits of working a wood-pile in this fashion are that it is quicker, there is less hassle with nets and the workload of the ferrets is reduced due to the efforts of the dogs. Most importantly, it has a good success rate with regard to catching rabbits.

I use two polecat hobs when hunting at woodpiles, and they invariably kill at least one rabbit that has been tardy about bolting. This does not stop them from pur-suing the other rabbits that are hiding in the wood. In this environment, where there is space for the ferrets to move around and over the rabbit, they are incredibly quick in their actions and the rabbit will be dead long before the ferreter can shift the wood to get to it.

The torch is a useful piece of equipment to have at hand in this working situation. It enables the ferreter to see further and more clearly into the woodpile than he is able to with the naked eye. The obvious benefits of using a torch are the ability to easily locate dead rabbits and observe the progress of the ferrets.

right animals at his disposal and can rely on them to cooperate with one another. This method relies on the efforts of the ferrets and terrier, or other rabbiting dogs, although nets are still used, but not in the same quantity as the first method. Firstly, place some nets over the most obvious-looking entry and exit points until between one third and one half of the woodpile is covered, and then enter the ferrets. Next, allow the dogs to work loose so that they can react to rabbit movement promptly and decisively. My terrier clambers freely over the woodpile and hopefully will get himself in the right position to deal with

USING A FERRET LOOSE ABOVE GROUND

Why Use a Ferret Above Ground?

The ferret is used loose above ground for essentially the same reason as it is entered into a warren, which is to make the rabbits bolt to a position where they can be caught either by a net or a dog. Some environments where a rabbit chooses to hide are above ground and inaccessible to dogs. In many cases the rabbit could easily be caught if it could be made to bolt. This is when the ferret can be indispensable, because wherever the rabbit hides the ferret can follow. By using my ferrets loose above ground, I can increase the number of rabbits that I catch at specific locations, and sometimes it is the only way to clear an area of rabbits. It also enables me to work my ferrets in a greater variety of environments. Since moving to Scotland, a lot of my ferreting takes place around old deserted farm buildings where there are a multitude of places for the rabbits to hide above ground. It should be remembered that the ferret is equally dreaded and feared by the rabbit above ground as it is in the warren.

Where to Use the Ferret Above Ground

The most likely location for ferreting above ground is on a farm and, in particular, around unused buildings that have fallen into a state of disrepair. There are usually items lying about, such as old doors and sheets of corrugated metal, which a rabbit is adept at using for cover. Similar materials, as well as fence posts, coils of old wire

and archaic agricultural machinery that are found lying in the ditches and alongside the hedges bordering farmers' fields, are also utilized by rabbits as a temporary refuge. Sometimes the rabbits build a small subterranean network of tunnels beneath these materials.

Working the Ferret Above Ground

The key to success when working above ground is a well-thought-out plan. The basis of such a plan is knowledge of the best position to release the ferret and the most likely place for the rabbit to bolt from. Sometimes these are not readily identifiable and can be ascertained only through trial and error, which in itself is a good learning experience. I have encountered many locations that, at first sight, have looked impossible to work. On these occasions I have learnt to stand back and take a few moments to consider the wider environment because, in a lot of cases, the best place to catch the rabbit is not in the immediate area where it is hiding. When assessing how to use the ferrets in this type of situation, the ferreter should consider the following factors:

1. Can nets be set in the immediate area where the rabbit is hiding?
2. In which direction is the rabbit likely to bolt and what destination will it head for? Keep a lookout for narrow, well-trodden pathways and small holes in hedges, walls or vegetation.
3. Identify any possible places along these paths where a net could be set, and also any suitable position for the terrier to launch an ambush from.
4. The location of the nearest warrens that the rabbit can escape to. Setting

nets over the holes of these warrens will catch the rabbit as it attempts to charge underground.

5. What does the ferreter wish his ferret to achieve? Sometimes the purpose may be to shift the rabbit to a location that can be more easily worked. This is a viable alternative to catching the rabbit straight away with a net or a dog.

6. The presence of any dangers to the ferret, ferreter or his dog.

There are many hazards around deserted farm buildings, such as containers that once held chemicals and rusty barbed wire. Once, while working my ferrets and dog at a derelict farmhouse and steading, I found a large slab on the ground near to some fallen posts under which rabbits routinely hide. On lifting the slab, I discovered that it was covering the opening of a deep well. This illustrates the need for the ferreter to be familiar with the environment in which his animals are expected to hunt.

The ferret can move at a rapid pace when loose and therefore requires constant, close supervision so that it does not wander to where the handler is unable to retrieve it. Working the ferret above ground requires a different approach to that undertaken at the warren, where the ferreter stands a safe distance away so as not to deter a rabbit from bolting. When my ferret is working loose, I follow behind him and stand next to any obstacles he goes under. I also allow my terrier to work freely in close

When working at warrens that lie in the ditches bordering a farmer's field, the easiest way to secure the net pegs is often to tie them to the lower strands of stock-proof fencing.

proximity to the ferret, and on numerous occasions they have driven rabbits into one another.

A ferret that gets plenty of loose exercise when it is not hunting responds best to this type of work, because it does not get over-excited when free from the confines of a run or the constraint of a lead. When above ground there is no need for the ferret to wear a collar with transmitter or be attached to a long line, which may quickly become entangled and be more of a hindrance than a help.

The ferret's hunting instinct is as keen above ground as it is in a warren. It can detect when rabbits are nearby and will drive them mercilessly from their makeshift hiding places. This may take some time depending on the area the rabbit has to move in as it tries to evade the ferret. For example, at one of my sites a corrugated metal roof from a barn has fallen to the floor, where it offers the rabbits 100ft^2 (9m^2) of space in which to move. The ferret may have to chase the rabbit around in circles for some time before it bolts. My terrier will patrol the edges of the roof where the gaps are biggest, because here he can grab a rabbit that has all its attention focused on evading the ferret.

When the rabbit does bolt or is caught by the dog, the ferret will emerge from the working site and sniff about in various directions as it tries to work out where the rabbit has gone. Sometimes the ferret may return under the obstacle where it has been hunting and retrace its steps as it tries to follow the trail of the rabbit. However, it will soon realize that there is no rabbit and, when it emerges, the handler should pick it up. Whenever possible there should be one person behind the ferret and another at a distance in front of it in the direction it is expected to travel.

The decision of where to work my ferret above ground is directly related to my terrier's ability to accurately indicate where the rabbits are, even though they are unseen. This enables me to release my ferret in the perfect location for it to commence its work. If a dog is not available, you can use the knowledge gained through observation of the nooks and crannies that the rabbits commonly hide in when they are above ground.

Hunting rabbits amongst the obstacles referred to in this section rarely involves the use of many purse nets. When there are obvious indications of where the rabbit will break cover, nets should be put

A terrier is an invaluable help to the ferret when working amongst rocks, woodpiles and gorse bushes.

in position. However, there are occasions when it is impossible to set nets around the obstacle under which the rabbit may be hiding. The obstacle may be inaccessible or it may not be possible to secure the net pegs or stretch out the purse net owing to the presence of objects for it to get caught on, such as the barbs of barbed wire. In these cases the best alternative is to set a net at a suitable point along the escape route that the rabbit will take. This may be as much as 10ft (3m) or 15ft (4.5m) away from the rabbit's hiding place. With this distance to cover there is a chance that the rabbit will ignore its established route, which is why I position the dogs close to the boundary of the rabbit's well-trodden path. The dogs will turn the rabbit back so that it has to either continue in the intended direction and into the net or retrace its steps, which will result in a confrontation with the ferret.

The best place to release the ferret when working amongst an assortment of farm rubbish is at the most unlikely place for the rabbit to bolt. The ferret will force the rabbit to use its common escape path, which is where the net or dogs are waiting.

FERRETING AT A WARREN LOCATED UNDER A GORSE BUSH

On many of the farms where I have ferreted, gorse is a common feature. It is found in locations that, for one reason or another, cannot be cultivated, such as between the stock-proof fencing that marks the boundaries of adjoining fields. As such, its growth is neither fashioned nor restrained by man and what was probably a long straight wall of hedge now grows in all directions.

It is an ideal place for the rabbits to take up residence. It offers abundant cover, a degree of protection from most predators and shelter from the weather. I have had occasion to crawl into the midst of a gorse bush when it was raining heavily and found that the moisture had barely penetrated the thorny canopy. Under the gorse, rabbits burrow underground and cut a network of interconnecting tunnels. By doing this they benefit from two lines of defence – the dense prickly gorse and the surface of the ground. Hunting the many rabbits living in these locations presents a number of problems.

The most obvious problem is access to the warren so that nets can be laid over the holes. Rabbits are not stupid; they dig very few holes on the periphery of the gorse where they can be reached easily. The majority of the holes are in the centre of the bush where they are difficult to reach. At one time gorse was used to stop heavy farm beasts straying from their fields, which indicates how impenetrable it can be. It might appear logical to cut the gorse back to give the ferreter access, but this would require a lot of work and destroy a favourable habitat for the rabbits, not to mention upsetting the farmer. When a warren is positioned beneath gorse, the terrier is unable to drive the rabbits from their cover in the same way he is accustomed to when they are sheltering in gorse bushes that are free from any diggings.

This type of working situation requires the combined efforts of the terrier and ferret, as well as some crafty setting of nets. The first thing to do is set nets over all the holes that can be reached. When this is done, stand well back from the gorse so that you can identify the small holes in the bush that are indicative of the path of a

Ferreting near trees may cause problems. The intertwined roots in the foreground will make digging difficult here.

rabbit run. Nets can then be set over these, which often requires resting the edges of the net on the branches of the gorse itself. I have caught a number of rabbits in this way. If possible, position a dog at either end of the gorse. They will either chase the rabbits back into the nets or into the path of one another.

When working a warren that is located in the midst of a thick gorse bush, there are three ways to enter the ferret. The first is to release the ferret at one end of the bush on the ground so that it can make its way freely and systematically towards the other end. The second option, which I favour, is to try and place the ferret as

close as possible to the main holes of the warren that lie at the centre of the bush. This is not always as easy as it sounds and usually involves much stretching and some crawling on all fours in order to release the ferret in the correct place. The plan is for the ferret to enter the warren at its epicentre and, in so doing, block this as an escape route and force the rabbits into bolting from the peripheral holes where dogs and nets lie in wait. The final option is to combine both of the aforementioned methods by using two ferrets: one ferret to work its way above ground through the gorse while the other is underground emptying the main chambers of the warren.

107

The experienced ferret can be relied upon to follow the rabbits and push them from their hiding places. I have never known my ferrets to linger under the bush once the rabbits have departed, but it is helpful if the ferret that is being worked will respond when it is called so that the ferreter can pick it up quickly. The rabbits that I have encountered in this type of setting have displayed a tendency to bolt rather than remain below ground when a ferret is pursuing them. This could, in part, be due to the fact that I am always careful to avoid overloading the warren with ferrets. It is also probably due to the abundance of cover that the rabbits have to hide and hop about in immediately above and around the warren. I usually keep my dogs back at this stage so that their presence will not deter the rabbits from following their familiar runs and bolting into the nets that have been set.

If the rabbits do persist in their evasion of the ferret and remain in the gorse for a prolonged period of time, the terrier is put to work and he will either drive them out or catch them at close quarters. Most terriers are an ideal size for pushing their way into the gorse and, when involved in hunting, will ignore the prickly spikes of the bush. The dog and ferret will need to work in close proximity to one another and therefore must be willing to work as a team and not display any animosity towards one another.

There is no quick way to get the ferret and terrier to accept one another and become friends. It is a task that requires time and patience, and it should only be undertaken after having first trained the dog and tamed the ferret. Once this has been achieved they can be introduced to one another. I usually do this by taking them for walks together, with the ferret

Sometimes the best way to catch a rabbit is to set a net at a strategic point along a rabbit's familiar escape route, which may lie a short distance away from where the rabbit is hiding. Look for small holes in walls and hedges accompanied by well-trodden paths leading to and from them.

being controlled by a long line so that it can be immediately checked if it tries to bite the dog. The terrier can be disciplined with voice commands.

The walks are repeated each day until both animals are accustomed to one another's presence. During these walks they are allowed to move right next to each other in order to test whether either of them still has an inclination to bite. When they have shown that there is no hint of hostility towards one another the ferret can be released from its lead. Both terriers and ferrets have playful dispositions, and it is not unusual to see them bounding about after one another. When a genuine relationship has developed between the terrier and the ferret, they will happily work and cooperate together, and recognize each other as a valuable ally in the hunt for rabbits. The terrier is clearly an indispensable member of the ferreting team and is particularly useful in awkward and unusual working environments. However, the dog will never be able to realize its potential unless the handler can trust it 100 per cent with his ferrets.

HOW TO KEEP AN EYE ON THE FERRET WHEN IT IS WORKING IN DIFFICULT ENVIRONMENTS

Whilst out ferreting one day at a site that is known locally as the 'quarry', I noticed that the rabbits were hiding in a huge mound of tangled gorse. On two sides the gorse is bordered by rocks, some of which are massive and help form a steep slope that I do not want my ferrets to enter. This is typical of many places that a ferreter will encounter, where it will not be easy to keep a watch on his ferret.

A large gorse bush offers the rabbits excellent protection and often the ferreter is only able to place nets over the periphery of the bush.

There are a number of reasons why it is vital for the ferreter to ensure that he can keep a close lookout for ferrets emerging from a warren. The first, and most obvious, is to enable the retrieval of the ferret, either to redirect its efforts or move on to another warren. Unfortunately, ferrets are not like dogs, which can be called back to the handler's side. The ferret will eventually need to be picked up. Another reason is to keep the ferret safe by preventing it from wandering into dangerous environments where the ferreter is unable to retrieve it. Thirdly, the appearance and movement of the ferret is an indicator of what is going on within the warren.

Difficult locations may be defined as warrens where the bolt holes cannot be observed from one position or where they are surrounded by heavy vegetation, bordered by rocks or near to a road. Even at a simple straightforward warren, the ferreter needs to remain observant. Admittedly, a bolting rabbit is usually followed by the ferret in close pursuit, in which case it can be easily retrieved. However, sometimes the unexpected happens. When my

brother and I were working an albino hob in a small, uncomplicated warren, it suddenly leapt out of a bolt hole and set off running. We thought that he would soon stop, but as he approached 30m with no slowing of pace we realized that we would have to intervene. We quickly pursued the runaway ferret with our dogs. One of the terriers managed to get in front of the ferret and we were able to grab him before he put himself in danger.

If ferreting by yourself, the best advice is to work those warrens where you are afforded a clear view of the bolt holes and surrounding ground. This will give you plenty of time to retrieve a ferret, even if it starts wandering about. I hunt at some warrens where I have an unhindered outlook for a considerable distance and, because the ferret is within sight, I am happy to let it walk about while I deal with the caught rabbit.

A lot of situations are not so easy and require watching from two or more vantage points in order to have all the bolt holes covered. These environments are best worked when the ferreter has someone

A folding saw is essential for making a tidy job when a branch of a hedge or a section of tree root needs removing.

else to help him. Not only can they help keep an eye out for the ferrets, they can also share the task of setting the nets.

Most awkward locations can be handled by two people. My brother and I employ a number of strategies to keep watch on our ferrets, and the positions that we assume depend upon the particular site being worked. The following sites are described as examples.

Where the whole of the site can be observed from two positions, we usually take responsibility for half the warren each. Often this will result in one of us watching the back while the other watches the front, but where the warren is square-shaped in layout, with bolt holes on all four sides, we position ourselves diagonally so that we can watch two sides of the warren each.

When the warren is bordered on one side by features such as heavy rocks that I do not want the ferret to enter, one of us watches the main part of the warren while the other takes responsibility for guarding those bolt holes nearest to the rocks so that any loose ferret can be retrieved

before it wanders off. This may result in just one of the ferreters doing the majority of the work, but at least we can keep the ferret out of danger. Similar positions are taken when working a warren that lies by a roadside. We also take the added precaution of only ferreting near to roads when the traffic is at its quietest.

Some sites, which lie on a slope such as the gorse mentioned at the beginning of this section, are so large and irregularly shaped that many bolt holes are obscured from view when trying to observe the warren from just two positions. In this situation, by moving back approximately 10m further than usual it was possible to see the majority, if not the whole, of the warren. However, as neither of us wanted to make a mad dash every time a rabbit bolted, we decided that one of us should stay close to the warren in a roving capacity under the direction of the one standing further away who could point to where the rabbits were bolting. With the benefit of an overview of the scene, the latter could note any appearance of the ferret above ground.

A ferret will be tired following a day's hunt and will appreciate a rest.

Using Dogs to Help Keep Lookout

The experienced rabbiting dog has its senses finely tuned to what is going on within and around the warren. My terrier always knows what is going to happen before I do. A prudent ferreter will utilize this ability, particularly when he is struggling to keep his eyes on a number of bolt holes at the same time. In order for the dog's skill to be effective, the ferreter needs to be able to accurately read the signals that the dog is displaying. I can tell by the posture, movement and sound that my dog makes when there is something happening at the bolt holes he is watching. His characteristics are so marked that it is quite easy to differentiate whether it is a rabbit bolting that has got his attention or the reappearance of the ferret from within the warren.

In order for the dog to be used as a lookout, it is essential that it remain in the 'stay' position for prolonged periods of time. You also need to decide whether to allow the dog to deal with the rabbits that are caught at the holes it is watching or whether the rabbits should be left alone until the ferreter arrives. This decision is usually dictated by the particular working environment itself, but the dog should be trained to respond to voice control at all times irrespective of what is decided. A dog that rushes to the warren to seize hold of every rabbit that it sees get caught in a net is a nuisance and will quickly prove to be more of a hindrance than a help. The ferreting dog must only get hold of rabbits that have been caught in nets when it has been given permission, and it should release its hold as soon as the command 'leave' is spoken.

The rabbiting terrier possesses acute hearing, sharp eyes, phenomenal scenting powers and lightning-quick reactions, and with careful training and some guidance these can prove to be an invaluable aid to the ferreter when he is undertaking such tasks as watching the warren.

Duties of the Ferreting Dog

- To detect where rabbits are hiding on the surface
- To drive rabbits underground into warrens
- To accurately mark the warrens that are inhabited
- To guard those holes that either cannot be netted or are difficult to see
- To catch any rabbits that evade the nets
- To aid the location of rabbits that are laid up within the warren
- To work happily alongside the ferret

CHAPTER 6

THE INFLUENCE OF THE WEATHER

As a sporting pursuit that takes place in the great outdoors, rabbiting with ferrets is obviously influenced by the prevailing weather conditions during the hunting season. The fact that traditional ferreting takes place during the coldest, wettest and windiest months of the year further emphasizes the effect that the weather can have on a day's ferreting. Having lived in various places throughout mainland Britain, I have noticed that the climate can alter significantly between different locations. Few can dispute that it is colder in the north and wetter in the west.

Other influential factors associated with climate are height above sea level and the presence of woodlands. For example, at higher altitudes the force of the wind is felt more keenly whereas a dense belt of trees will greatly reduce the force of the wind. Consequently, the information in this chapter should be taken in conjunction with an awareness of your local climate and the typical weather conditions you are likely to experience at the sites where you hunt. I now reside in the northeast of Scotland, known as the cold shoulder of the country, which has the most challenging weather for ferreting that I have known.

The ferreter will find it beneficial to listen to a weather forecast for the day he is planning to go hunting. If you have a variety of sites to choose from, the forecast will influence which one you select. For example, I choose sheltered ground when it is wet and windy and exposed sites when there is frost on the ground or plenty of sunshine. The ever-changing winter weather provides plenty of opportunities to hunt all the different sites during the season. I am not implying that you cannot hunt certain locations in particular weather, but choosing a specific site in certain conditions does make the task of ferreting easier and more comfortable.

Knowing whether the weather is going to be fair or foul will enable the ferreter to select the appropriate equipment for the conditions, for example nylon or hemp nets for wet or dry weather respectively. Obviously, you need to dress according to the weather conditions.

The rabbit is also influenced by the weather and will alter its behaviour according to the conditions. For instance, on a warm sunny morning the rabbit is more likely to be seen above ground in open spaces than when it is raining heavily or excessively windy. Being out in all types of weather and overcoming the challenges that are presented is part of the fun of ferreting.

FERRETING IN FINE WEATHER

The Ferreter

Most ferreters would describe a dry day with sun and no wind as the perfect weather for ferreting. All the tasks associated with ferreting, from setting nets to digging, are easier to perform in dry weather and any location, from exposed hillside to woodland, can be hunted. This type of weather is suitable for a long day's

ferreting in which large difficult warrens can be worked, in particular those that are likely to involve a complicated dig.

The Ferret

The ferret can tolerate warm temperatures and will not be bothered by the hottest days that occur during the traditional rabbiting season. However, simple measures can be taken to improve the ferret's comfort when temperatures are high:

• Only place a small amount of straw in your carrying device, whether it is a box or a bag.
• Do not leave your carrier with the ferret inside in a position that is exposed to the sun. If the box or bag

A purpose-built carrying box for warmer days. The large mesh front gives extra ventilation.

114

is to be left on the ground for a prolonged period of time, always put it in a sheltered place.

- Offer your ferret a drink of water at regular intervals. Most ferreters carry a flask and take a break from working the ferrets so that they can have a refreshing cup of tea or coffee. It is good practice to give the ferret a drink at the same time.
- You can use a carrying box that has been specially made for use in dry weather. This has a larger portion of wire incorporated into its design than a conventional carrying box and is, as a bonus, very light to carry. Alternatively, if you carry your ferrets in a bag, you can easily make additional breather holes.

My ferrets enjoy hunting in fine weather and do not seem to physically tire any quicker than they do on cooler days.

The Rabbit

Rabbits, like many humans, are inclined to indulge themselves when the sun is shining brightly. They emerge from their warrens and brazenly sit in the sun when they are confident that there is no threat to them nearby. The ferreter will encounter many more rabbits above ground on a dry sunny day than he will on a wet one. They are more likely to nestle down in the long grass or linger at the base of hedges or gorse bushes than spend time in the warren.

This would suggest that dry sunny weather is not ideal for ferreting. However, with some effort the rabbits can be located lurking above ground and persuaded to bolt towards the nearby

warrens. The most successful and reliable way to do this is with a dog, which uses its scenting powers to search all the hedges, bushes and other likely hiding places. This is the type of work that terriers, in particular, excel at and enjoy. If you do not have a dog, you can use your own presence to prompt the rabbits that are above ground to bolt. First identify the places the rabbits usually frequent when they are not down the warrens and then walk your way systematically through them. The majority of rabbits will grow uncomfortable when a person gets too near to them. Their instinct to run will become so strong that they will make a dash for the nearest warren. Inevitably, some places that rabbits use as temporary cover cannot be penetrated by either the ferreter or his dogs. In such cases I release my ferret and let it work its way through these refuges. The unexpected presence of a ferret in a tight spot above ground will rapidly persuade the rabbits to run.

FERRETING IN WET WEATHER

The Ferreter

Wherever you live in the British Isles, rain will be a feature of the winter weather. When combined with strong winds, the effects of the rain are intensified. In his book, *Rabbiting*, Bob Smithson states that wet-weather ferreting is not worth the bother. His view is that the ferreter will be uncomfortable kneeling on the ground and the purse nets will become waterlogged and hard to handle. As you would expect from an experienced

A ferret should be given a drink at regular intervals when working.

countryman, these are valid points. However, one of my eccentricities is a liking for being out in the rain, whether for a cross-country run, walking the dog or rabbiting with the ferrets. As a result, I have discovered that measures can be taken to counteract the problems highlighted by Mr Smithson.

Strong rain can quickly demoralize a person if he is not prepared for it, and in such situations the overwhelming desire is to get home as soon as possible. Indisputably, the best way to combat fierce rain is to wear the appropriate clothing. In order to hunt rabbits in persistent rain, the ferreter should wear waterproof clothing from head to toe. There are certain garments that I use year after year, which enable me to ferret comfortably all day long in the pouring rain. They include a waxproof cap for wet, windy weather and a wide-brimmed leather Rogue hat, as worn by South African hunters, for wet, still conditions. When it is wet and cold I wear a British-made tweed coat, but when hot I use a Gore-Tex army parka with no lining. If there is any likelihood of encountering sharp or rough obstacles I wear waxproof leggings, which are resistant to tearing as well as being thoroughly waterproof. Otherwise I wear a pair of Deerhunter Montana trousers, which are waterproof and have a high back that is ideal for the ferreter who has to bend a lot to set nets. In wet, muddy conditions I wear wellingtons, but in all other wet weather conditions I prefer a Gore-Tex-lined walking-style boot.

I always use nylon nets in wet weather because even if the net is not dried properly it will not rot. Good-quality hemp tends to soak up more moisture and, as a result, becomes heavier than nylon. My favourite net for rainy days is made of 6z spun nylon because it remains soft to handle and does not tangle when wet.

If the weather is wet and you have a choice of hunting site, choose those that offer shelter in the form of hedges, trees, walls or buildings. I avoid those warrens that may involve a lengthy dig when they are worked and also those that are located in a ditch or near to a stream. In heavy rain, if it becomes necessary to dig, the earth will turn to mud and make the warren as slippery as an ice rink. A small stream, which may look harmless and picturesque, can swell at an alarming rate and put your ferret in danger.

The Ferret

A ferret is not deterred by heavy rainfall. It will be hunting mainly within the warren where the conditions are quite different from those experienced by the ferreter who is above ground. One of the reasons why rabbits build warrens is to provide a secure home that protects them from the weather. I have dug into a warren on a wet day and found that its inner chambers are perfectly dry.

A standard carrying box will provide the ferret with suitable protection from the rain when it is being transported from warren to warren. If you use a carry bag to transport the ferret, place it in a secondary

To be comfortable when ferreting during the winter it is necessary to wear the appropriate clothing to combat the weather.

carrier to protect it. I put mine in the top of an open rucksack, which allows plenty of air to get to the ferret and keeps the rain off the carry bag.

The Rabbit

A healthy rabbit has a fine coat of fur consisting of an outer and inner layer, and

117

is capable of enduring severe weather. However, rabbits will seek shelter from the rain, and therefore wet weather is good for ferreting because the rabbits are more likely to be found within the warren than sitting on the surface. Rabbits do not appear to be any more reluctant to bolt from the warren in wet conditions.

FERRETING IN WINDY WEATHER

The Ferreter

In Scotland, where I live, wind is common throughout the year, although it occurs with more regularity and is stronger during the winter months. I have had to learn the best way to employ the ferreting technique in what are probably the worst conditions in which to practise the sport.

The wind is a nuisance when ferreting for the following reasons:

- It disturbs nets that have been carefully set and often blows them so that they no longer cover the entire hole, making them ineffective.
- It makes communication with other ferreters and the dogs more difficult.
- It has a deafening effect, which makes it hard for the ferreter to listen for the tell-tale noises of rabbit movement within the warren.
- If the wind is accompanying rain or snow it makes these conditions feel more severe. This can make standing waiting for a bolt a very unpleasant experience.

Can anything be done to overcome these problems and lessen the devastating effects of the wind on a ferreter's rabbit hunting efforts? Fortunately, the answer is 'yes', and the solutions are not too difficult to achieve. Let us look at each of these in turn.

Finding a way to stop the nets being moved by the wind is of primary importance. When ferreting in windy conditions,

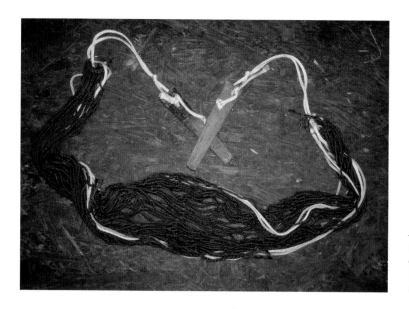

A handmade purse net with a peg at either end. It is intended for use in windy conditions.

if possible choose warrens that benefit from natural or man-made shelter. When there is no alternative to working a warren that leaves your nets exposed to the wind, the nets must be held in position in such a way that the nets are not prevented from freely running along the drawcords and pursing properly around the rabbits. I recommend using heavy nets, for example 6z spun nylon nets, 7-ply hemp nets or 10z machine-made nylon nets. If you make your own or buy handmade nets, try using double-twined nets, which should be twice the weight of a normal net.

When the ground is soft it is possible to push the edges of the net into the ground at intervals along the drawcords. However, this will not work in fierce winds, and the nets will need to be held down more firmly. There are two methods for doing this. The first is to use something to hold the edge of the net down so that it retains its position as the wind blows. Whatever is used must release its hold as soon as the rabbit hits the net with any force so that it can purse around the animal. Heavy gauge wire, approximately 8cm long, can be bent double to give an inverted 'V' shape with sides measuring 4cm. These can be pushed into the ground about half their length at strategic points along the edges of the net. Only four of these holders should be needed and they can be placed opposite one another at the upper and lower quadrants of the round purse net.

Alternatively, the ferreter could employ a net that has two pegs connected to it, such as the French 'bourse' nets, which have a peg at either end. This provides two anchor points, which help to keep the net in position.

Most ferreters make a minimum of noise when working a warren because they believe that noise will deter the rabbits from bolting. Ferreters use their own idiosyncratic form of sign language to relay important information to one another, and this is especially useful in windy conditions. Hand signals can also be used instead of the voice to direct a suitably trained dog.

The inability to hear obvious noises relating to rabbit movement from within the warren should not prove to be too great a disadvantage. The ferreter must trust his ferrets and wait patiently for the results of their subterranean hunting. I have learnt to watch my dog because he has more sensitive hearing than I do and is capable of monitoring any noise that originates from the warren. By correctly interpreting his posture and gestures, I have some idea of what is happening within the warren.

Ferreting can, at times, be a static sport, and it is a good idea to wear clothing that is proven to be windproof when out ferreting all day in the cold wind.

The Ferret

The wind has little influence on the ferret's work underground, where the effects of strong wind are barely felt. Even though the nets are prone to movement by the wind, my ferrets are still able to pass through the mesh spaces of the net without causing any disturbance to it.

The Rabbit

In strong wind, rabbits will seek some form of shelter, which is most likely to be a warren. Some ferreters have suggested that rabbits are more reluctant to bolt in windy conditions than they would normally be. This may be because they can see the slight movement of the net caused by the wind and are uneasy about exiting the warren. Also, the noise created by strong wind may confuse the rabbit so that it is slower to respond to the threat of the ferret in the warren.

FERRETING IN THE SNOW

The Ferreter

The depth of the snow will indicate whether it is viable to use ferrets to hunt rabbits. Anything less than 8in (20cm) may be workable. When snow is on the road it is preferable to concentrate on warrens that are close to home and ideally those that are within walking distance. A heavy snowfall will prevent the ferreter:

- finding the bolt holes
- reaching the ground to secure the net pegs
- travelling to the warrens.

Snowfall of up to 4in (10cm) poses few problems for the ferreter. The warrens are easy to see and the holes will not be blocked with snow. Furthermore, the rabbits' whereabouts are revealed by the tracks in the snow. When the snowfall is between 4in and 8in (10cm and 20cm) ferreting is more difficult. Many of the holes will be filled with snow and securing the net pegs can be difficult and time-consuming.

I have found that unless the snow is about 12in (30cm) deep it rarely covers all the holes of a single warren that is located on a slope or has sides facing in different directions. Usually, one aspect of the

Ferrets are happy to work when snow is on the ground.

warren has more protection from the snow and, as a result, the holes do not become blocked. This effect can also be caused by the prevailing wind when the snow was falling or the subsequent drift when it was on the ground.

Even when there has been heavy snow and most of my usual warrens are unworkable, I always have a reserve number of warrens to use. These warrens are located within a walled area where trees cast their shadow over the warrens. This combination of man-made and natural shelter offers the warrens a unique and well-protected environment.

Snow can hide obstacles and hazards on the ground, and therefore it is safer for the ferreter to stay on land that he knows well. The ferreter should also ensure that he has the appropriate clothing, paying particular attention to footwear that offers warmth, dryness and, most vitally, grip.

Snow can soak the nets and make them heavy, which is why I always use nylon nets. Unlike hemp, they absorb little moisture and will not rot if they are not dried properly.

Unless the snow has been exceptionally heavy, or drifted, it rarely blocks all the holes of a large rabbit warren.

The warren located in the centre of this picture is protected by bushes and a stone wall, which makes it an ideal site to hunt at in bad weather conditions.

The Ferret

Ferrets like the snow and enjoy rubbing about and playing in it. They certainly have no aversion to hunting rabbits in the snow. I always take care to not enter too many ferrets to a snowbound warren in order to avoid having to dig. Although it is possible to dig in the snow, the task is more difficult and time-consuming. The ferret will get very wet in the snow and the ferreter should make sure that there is plenty of dry straw in the carrying box or bag. A small towel, carried in the game bag, can be used to dry the ferret, which will prevent it suffering from any chills.

The Rabbit

Rabbits are well equipped to cope with the snow. Even when their homes become snowbound, they can survive without food for several days thanks to their unusual digestive system. They are also good diggers and can clear their way through the snow with relative ease. When the

Rabbits should be hung conveniently out of the way while other warrens are being worked. A branch of a nearby tree is perfect for this.

When there are no trees nearby, a rabbit can be hung over a spade that has been pushed into the ground to hold it steady.

snowfall is heavy and grass is unavailable, the rabbits are likely to eat the bark and shoots of young trees and bushes. If the snow is thin on the ground, the rabbits may scrape it out of the way so that they can reach the grass.

Rabbits do leave the warren and move about over the snow, principally for the purpose of foraging and not for play or exercise. Consequently, when snow is on the ground, the rabbits will usually be in the warren, but they will bolt when pursued by a ferret. Because some of the holes will be blocked with snow, the warren has less escape routes than normal for the rabbit. I have never seen a rabbit burst or dig its way out through a snow-filled bolt hole. They always make for the holes that are already clear of snow, which suits the ferreter because these are the only holes that he is able to see to put nets over.

Transporting rabbits on the end of a walking stick.

A small number of rabbits can be carried in a roe sack.

Rabbits attached to a strap or rope that is slung over the shoulder.

Rabbits tied to the straps of a rucksack.

Rabbits can be draped over a pony, which is how the old Pembrokeshire rabbit catchers carried their rabbits.

125

Ferreting in the Frost

Frost presents few problems to the ferreter, ferret or rabbit and it has little effect on hunting. Some ferreters, however, believe that the crunch of the frost when a person walks over it can be heard by the rabbits below ground, which makes them reluctant to leave the warren. The only difficulty that I have encountered due to frost-hardened ground has been pushing in the net pegs. This is easily overcome by using a mallet to drive the pegs in (*see* pages 36 and 70).

On my way home after a successful morning's ferreting.

FURTHER READING

For information on ferrets and how to look after them:

Bezzant, D. *Ferreting – A Traditional Country Pursuit* (The Crowood Press, 2004)
Porter, V. and Brown, N. *The Complete Book of Ferrets* (Pelham Books, 1985)
Plummer, D.B. *Modern Ferreting* (Boydell, 1977)

For comprehensive details on how to make purse nets:

Glynn, H.G. *Net-making for Sport* (Tideline Books, 1989)

USEFUL ADDRESSES AND CONTACTS

Ferreting organization dedicated to promoting ferreting and ferrets throughout the UK:
National Ferreter's Register, www.ferreting.biz

For purse nets and other ferreting equipment:
KP&S Nets, Lodge House, Buckland St Mary, Chard, Somerset TA20 3TA. Tel: 0845 6036861

For Buck knives as featured on page 42:
Whitby & Co. Tel: 01539 721032

Suppliers of game bags, rucksacks, drinks bottles, flasks and clothing:
Jack Pyke of England. Tel: 01234 740327

For leather fingerless gloves:
Viper. Tel: 01234 740327

For walking boots like the Irish Setter 869 as featured on page 50:
Foot Fetish. Tel: 01297 34616

For army surplus clothing:
flecktarn.co.uk. Tel: 01276 855995

INDEX